EMBODIMENT
– Moving beyond mindfulness

"Mark is the boldest embodiment facilitator out there."
— *Adam Wilder, founder of the Togetherness Festival*

"Mark Walsh brings embodiment to life with passion, irreverence, and grit. It makes a body want to celebrate!"
— *Ginny Whitelaw Roshi, CEO, Institute for Zen Leadership*

"Although explicitly a technical book, in reading it one senses that Mark has lived his understanding from the inside out. The content of the book itself is his own embodiment. Brilliant!!"
— *Guy Sengstock, co-founder of Circling*

"Mark has written a down to earth accessible classic that's much needed in our often numb world. Let's face it, sometimes he is a twat yes; but I'm an ex rock star and this book is marginally better than groupie sex, drugs and rock 'n roll."
— *Jamie Catto, film-maker (One Giant Leap), author,*
workshop leader, ex Faithless singer

"Fun, accessible, fresh, while still grounded and full of profound insight, *Embodiment* is a must-read for all humans."
— *Jessica Graham, author of "Good Sex: Getting Off Without Checking Out"*

"A brilliant book, distilling decades of embodied exploration with a unique blend of wisdom, wit, irreverence, and humour."
— *Joel & Michelle Levey, founders of Wisdom at Work,*
authors of "Mindfulness, Meditation, and Mind Fitness"

"I love Mark's book! It is not a treatise but a poetic call to remember what it is like to be embodied. The mixture of the lyricism with clear educational practicality is exactly what is needed to get people to return to the body"
— *John Vervaeke, Psychology and Cognitive Science Department,*
University of Toronto, author of "Awakening from the Meaning Crisis"

"The must-read book of the year in the Embodiment field. It offers a compelling, well informed, humorous and at times poetic feast of "tapas" to delight all appetites. Mark's practical wisdom has helped deepen my own embodied leadership and I highly recommend this powerful work to every other leader."
— *Dr Lynne Sedgmore CBE, former CEO of the Centre for Excellence*
in Leadership, leadership coach and interfaith minister

"Mark Walsh offers a comprehensive overview of embodiment that is practical and empowering, and offers a platform from which this emergent field can and will continue to evolve. Embodiment is exciting, passionate, and useful!"
— *Mariana Caplan, PhD., MFT author of "Yoga & Psyche:*
Integrating Yoga and Psychology for Healing"

"Mark has decades of experience in developing practical activities and principles for discovering embodiment. He has generously shared them in this easy-to-read yet expansive book."

– Martha Eddy, director of Dynamic Embodiment

"This offering is less a book and more a string of pearls. It is a series of one page essays and poems that explain how cruelties arise out of body numbness. What is new and important in Mark's book is his courageous description of his use of embodiment practices as part of his own work to heal his childhood traumas."

– Paul Linden, PhD, aikido 6th dan, author, founder of
Being In Movement® Mindbody Education

"*Embodiment* is very much a cut-the-crap book, charged with poetry, iconoclasm, personal anecdote, and a passion for helping us all recognise the sacred aliveness of the body's intelligence. If you feel disconnected, if you yearn to return to a deeper truth in your life, pick this book up and welcome its provocations!"

– Philip Shepherd, author of "Radical Wholeness" and "New Self, New World"

"Classic Mark Walsh! A collection of decidedly irreverent pithy, probing critiques of our culture-wide dissociation from our bodies. Enjoy!"

– Roger Walsh (no relation), MD, PhD, author of
"Essential Spirituality: The Seven Central Practices"

"Mark is a man of big vision and powerful intentionality for bringing the great benefits of embodiment into the world. I am grateful for this offering. Enjoy!"

– Russell Delman, founder of The Embodied Life School

In *Embodiment*, Mark gives voice to a joyous, angry, sensual war-cry – the body ferociously reclaiming its primacy in a disembodied world.

– Terry Patten, author, "A New Republic of the Heart",
co-author "Integral Life Practice"

"This book offers a comprehensive view of the embodiment territory. The stories and suggestions range from raucous and racy, to tender and touching. There is food for thought and a plethora of helpful hints for student and facilitator alike."

– Wendy Palmer, author of "Leadership Embodiment"

EMBODIMENT
– Moving beyond mindfulness

MARK WALSH

Unicorn Slayer Press

First published 2020, by Unicorn Slayer Press

© 2020 Mark Walsh

ISBN: 978-1-9162492-2-6 (pbk)
ISBN: 978-1-9162492-1-9 (ebk)

This book is dedicated to all those that created the work that I love: Paul Linden, Francis Briers and Alexandra Vilvovskaya particularly, for their service on the Embodied Facilitator Course. And also, of course, the woman/mystery cat-creature, whose embodiment feels most like home.

CONTENTS

This is why embodiment is trending right now: the times necessitate it.

- In times of chaos, the body is an anchor.
- In times of mistrust and "post-truth", the body is a source of wisdom.
- In a time of disconnection, the body is where reconnecting begins. First to ourselves, then through that to meaning, then each other, and vitally, to the planet.

ACKNOWLEDGEMENTS

Standing in the ruins of writing this book, at midnight on the publication deadline, I find myself compelled to return to the acknowledgments. Writing this book took everything I had to give, and I am now satisfied that it is my best effort. There was literally blood, sweat and tears on the pages on many occasions; and I had to break and reform myself several times to finish it. The effort however was not solo, and there are many to thank.

I would firstly like to acknowledge the Embodied Yoga Principles (EYP) and Embodied Facilitator Course (EFC) communities for being the supportive laboratory for this book. Everything here has been tried, tested and developed in these communities in the UK and in Russia, as well as in workshops in over thirty countries. EFC UK co-founder Francis Briers was especially central to EFC's development and worked closely with me to develop several of the models in this book, and Alexandra Vilvovskaya has clarified many of them with her Russian elegance. The EFC tribe as a whole, though, has been the vibrant, playful, intense peer-learning crucible where our integrations and innovations have occurred, and hundreds of people have played a part. My close EYP colleague and friend Vidyadasa has also been instrumental and a huge support emotionally, more times than I can remember, and the ever-patient Catherine O'Mahony has held it together for many years with her frankly scary organisation and Walsh-whispering skills.

My gratitude also goes to my primary influences in the field of embodiment. Paul Linden has been a loving second father to me and has shown me that what really matters is kindness. He is perhaps the biggest single influence on me and the only one that I hold a direct lineage relationship with. Wendy Palmer of Leadership Embodiment and Richard Strozzi-Heckler (who led the way with working with the body in business and coaching are two big influences). Other major embodied facilitation inspirations that I would like to acknowledge include Stuart Heller, Ginny Whitelaw and Dylan Newcomb, all legends in this field and on whose shoulders this book stands.

I have had innumerable teachers in many body practices, but I would like to thank in particular: William Smith Shihan OBE, Philip Smith Shihan, and the Ren Shin Kan senior teachers, Don Levine (who saw potential in me when this was not obvious), Miles Kessler, and Tom and Maria Helsby from aikido. Also, Shinzen Young, Junpo Denis Kelly Roshi, The Thai Forest Sangha and Rob Burbea from meditation. In dance, I could name many tango teachers, contact improv teachers, and conscious dance teachers, though Adam Barley is a long-time friend and warrants a special mention. From yoga: Peter Blackaby, Gary Carter and Jim Tarren. From body therapy: Michael Soth, Russell Rose, and Beverly Nolan. From comedy improv: my EFC colleagues Rachel Blackman and Liz Peters, and Maydays founder John Cremer.

Acknowledgements go to the elders of the field of embodiment, who have contributed to building the somatic cathedral that exists today: Don Hanlon Johnson, George Leonard, Michael Murphy, Bonnie Bainbridge-Cohen, and Anna Halprin to name but a few hugely respected figures. I could also mention the teachers of my teachers, such as Moshe Feldenkrais, Ida Rolf, Thomas Hanna, Matthias Alexander . . . but then we'd be into a history book! Suffice to say the embodiment field, while only just starting to come together, has been built upon the hard work of many lives.

The book itself is of course also a labour of many minds and hands especially my PA Agi, and also designer Matt, Karen "The Book Mentor" Williams, editors Wendy and Amber, numerous proofreaders and hundreds of people on Facebook (in some ways actually this book is a product of modern community "group-mind" and online co-creation, unlike books of old). They all played their part. Please forgive me for not mentioning you all by name! As ever, it takes a village, and I understand why artists in many eras did not sign their work, as viewed through lenses of practicality, embodied interrelationality and spirituality, the idea of having one name on the cover is absurd.

THE GENTLE REVOLUTION OF COMING HOME TO THE BODY

Welcome to the gentle revolution of coming home to the body. That's all "embodiment" is: returning to our humanity – and that's huge. The hour is late, the need is great, and a book is . . . just a book, but it's a start that's sorely needed. I dream of a world where cycles of numbing and violence are broken, where the cruelties of unfeeling abusers are imaginable, and where we care for each other and the planet as easily as we breathe. This vision is not just a possibility, but an inevitability as the wave of embodiment surges. In a cynical world to have such hopes may seem naive, but I see that a "movement movement" is firmly afoot.

This book consists of several years of thoughts, blogs, poems and social media posts assembled into something approaching a meaningful order. There are box-outs describing some of the most important embodied experiences of my life, so it's deeply personal too. It is somewhat non-linear in nature, as is embodiment. There's repetition and randomness, and it's a beautiful, mildly chaotic collage! For this reason, it can be dipped into freely, and many seemingly "light" sections will deepen with rereading. Any book on embodiment is, of course, ridiculous if not put to practical use, so I'd encourage you to practise what's offered within, engage with it personally, dance with it, read it to your lover in bed, whatever. To use a restaurant analogy: eat the food (the practices), not the menu (the words pointing to them).

For those seeking more structured and specific offerings about embodiment or related professional skills, please see later chapters and the resources at the back of this book. Otherwise, feast on the tapas[1] of bodily musings here.

Embodiment is a birthright, a wild ride and a gentle but (make no mistake) revolutionary adventure of becoming. Enjoy.

THE BODY OF LOVE

– Long Road Sixth Form College, Cambridge, UK

I'm 16. A golden sun is sinking as we walk hand in hand into the little patch of woodland tucked behind our college. Light is shining through the trees and through us. Her hand is soft and alive, feeling into me. We leave the functional modernist classrooms behind – square boxes of banality.

We spend a long time just standing close, appreciating each other through the heart and the senses. Both nervous and awestruck. I nestle my face in her long dark hair, smelling the blossom, and time dies. There are no words.

It's the first day of Spring and we kiss our first kiss. It's not like anything I've experienced. Sally's my first love, and a gateway to something much bigger. We melt. I hold her as the most precious, beautiful person in the world. I lose where she ends and I begin. No bodily borders, no embodied boundaries – we dissolve into each other. I lose myself, gain everything. Union. One taste.

There's light shining out of us and it's good. I'm alive for the first time in my life. Life! – gushing through our bodies like a river of electric pleasure. I feel whole, unified with her, myself and the divine – a stranger no longer. I'm home. I disappear. I can't express it, words are too blunt.

Two weeks later we sleep together for the first time and become love and luminosity itself. The body opens as a mystic door and life is never quite the same again. I am already forever grateful, and already know that I'll lose her. Again. And again.

---

1 A meal of many small dishes found in Spain.

CHAPTER 1

THE DISEMBODIED MESS THAT WE'RE IN

This book follows a simple structure:

I'll give you my take on why we're screwed up and how disembodiment is a root cause of that. I'll describe what embodiment is and the solutions it offers. I'll suggest simple practical tools. I'll offer some real-life applications, and illustrate it all with some personal stories. I'll state some things that can go wrong with this set of solutions.

So, there's a logical structure here, but feel free to jump around or read one or two random bits each day, if you prefer. I'm imagining some of you will read this on the toilet, in fact a perfectly relaxing embodied location – inspiration in, crap out. Ahh.

Embodiment will be defined in detail shortly. For now, "dis-embodied" can just be taken to mean being disconnected from our bodies: cut off from ourselves.

So, let's begin.

WHY BOTHER WITH EMBODIMENT?

When we start to see the body as the most accessible aspect of ourselves, we are profoundly empowered. We gain access to our own "operating system". We can know ourselves to a new depth, can change our state and develop our being. We cease to be victims. We connect to and influence others more effectively. We become more ethical. Simply and profoundly, we reclaim our humanity and our birthright by coming back home.

TEN REASONS YOU MIGHT WANT TO DEVELOP YOUR EMBODIMENT

- To know what is blindingly obvious to everyone else about you
- To have a choice in how you are
- To manage your neurotic insanity and out-of-control emotions
- To be a bit less of an arsehole, a bit more of the time
- To be a more compelling leader, more sensitive parent, or more vibrant lover
- To heal the shit that your parents couldn't so that you don't pass it on
- To have more fun and deepen EVERY pleasure. Really, it all gets better
- To stop making everything so bloody complicated and start enjoying the simplicity of relationships
- To be more creative
- To tune into a clearer sense of life purpose

SEVEN MORE . . .

- To feel deeply at home in your own skin. To have a bodily sense of belonging
- To play more freely with children, of all ages
- To get unhooked from addictions, large and small
- To be better connected to your own needs and values, to be less easily pushed around by others' agendas
- To be more sexually attractive in a way that has nothing to do with your physique or standard societal beauty norms
- To (and screw every cynic who has given up on this) make the world at least a little bit better
- To feel fully alive, and to be fully human

Now, I'm quite aware this may all sound too good to be true, and embodiment isn't a miracle cure, but all this is true. I go into most of the above points in detail throughout the book. Don't believe me, do the work and find out for yourself.

THE TEN FS: EMBODIED ESSENTIALS

Here are ten embodied essentials required to function well as a human animal, and some practices that build them:

1. Feeling (mindfulness, emotional awareness, intuitive practices)
2. Freeing (self-regulation, e.g. centring, and deeper body therapy)
3. Friending (embodied connection, authenticity, empathy, leadership)
4. Fighting (martial arts)
5. Fixing (healing arts, bodywork)
6. Fleeing (running, parkour)
7. Fucking (romance, seduction, tantra)
8. Frolicking (humour, play and improv practices)
9. Funking (free dance, expressive arts)[2]
10. Feeding (restorative, sleep, breath and food practices)

How many of these are you skilled in?

Thanks to Rafe Kelley and Ido Portal for the idea for this list.

HOW I KNOW IF I'M CUT OFF FROM MY BODY

Even as an embodiment professional with a life-long practice, I find myself losing touch with my body regularly. It's easy to judge oneself for this, but this doesn't help, and it's hardly surprising, really, given the world that we live in – so we should all probably cut ourselves some slack.

Losing touch with oneself is *state disembodiment* and the quicker we can notice this and come back, the better. "The power is in the recovery", as embodiment teacher Wendy Palmer says. I find it helpful to note certain red flags that indicate it's time to log off and get my yoga mat out, or just slow down and feel for a moment. Usually the journey is from noticing I'm not noticing, to noticing discomfort and, eventually, noticing the relief in coming home.

---

2 Could also potentially be called "flow".

SO, WHAT ARE THESE RED FLAGS?

Here are some:

- I notice that I'm not noticing my body (but this is tricky: how do you feel not feeling?)
- My posture is not balanced
- I'm brutalising myself with overwork, treating myself like an industrial machine
- My breathing is tight and irregular
- My body aches from tension (especially back, shoulders and belly) or is exhausted. This can feel like coming back to a resentful angry child who has been left alone too long
- I'm rushing. It is possible to be embodied fast (as in martial arts) but rushing skips feeling
- I have a hot "electric" feeling in my head and face
- I stop listening
- I'm eating low quality food, especially when not hungry, or engaging in other addictive behaviours to self-regulate
- I'm hurting myself in subtle or less subtle ways in order to feel
- I have numbness to strong stimuli, like loud music, strong tastes, etc
- There's a subtle, overall feeling of contraction and limitation in the whole body, like being in a cage, a loss of natural expansiveness
- I'm ungrateful
- I'm treating others as sex or success objects – as means to an end[3]

---

3 Credit to my Russian embodiment colleague Tonya Osipova for the idea for this list.

THE BODY OF HATE

– Cambridge, UK

I'm 18. I storm out of the pub into a stormy night. Rain hisses like vipers on my flaming skin. I'm napalm. I'm rage incarnate. I'm hurt and I want to hurt. I could gouge out The Buddha's eyes. I'm not a violent man.

Everything is clenched; my eyes are daggers looking to taste blood. My mind is entangled, trying to process what I've just been accused of. I focus on the anger to block it out. I'm dragon's breath; I'm Satan's claws.

Around me are the sounds of a Friday night in a gentrified student town. I don't hear them. I know he's followed behind as I demanded, when I turned over the table inside like Jesus' sick brother. He's angry too. She also followed and is weeping. Not the first time I've made the person I care most about cry. Her long dark hair is a mess, in the rain and tears . . . but she's still my definition of beauty. If I was thinking now, I'd ask her to forgive me and walk away. I'm not a violent man.

She pleads as her new boyfriend and I square up. We're not violent men.

She runs off into the night, body collapsing and twisting. Everyone has a limit. When she left me for him – a friend – I wasn't at my limit yet. I understood, in my head at least, that it sometimes happens and that you can't control people's hearts. Tonight though, I've been pushed through that wall. Months of pain have just found an outlet. First-hate cuts deep. The alcohol and amphetamines don't help, but even without them I'd still be mindless, soulless, and far from my centre.

The "fight", if you can call it that, is over in a few seconds. It was a pathetic scuffle really. Neither of us knows how to fight yet; we're not violent men.

Mutual friends pulled us off each other. The hardest punch of the night was landed on the back of my head by someone who claimed to know us, but was probably just drunk and wanted trouble. I went home, rocking and crying in the back of a friend's car. My balls were up near my throat and I won't sleep for days. I'm not a violent man.

The next day was my best friend James' birthday and he was having a party as eighteen-year-olds are inclined to. My own was a few days ago – I am now officially a man . . . violent or otherwise. I celebrated the arrival of adulthood – what a joke – with the handful of people who stubbornly care for me, despite how I've been behaving lately. I got unconsciously drunk, as I did every night. A photo from then shows me skinny, shaven headed with a mad self-destructive look in my eye, with friends looking on not knowing how to help. It had been a bad summer. When not working in the Victorian conditions of an industrial corporate farm, I argued furiously with my parents, as they did with each other. Simply, I wasn't happy. I missed her like the sky misses the wind, and needed to get the hell out of inbred-Dodge. Life in rural East Anglia, and with my disintegrating family, was already over. I needed to escape, I sought something . . . more . . . deeper . . .

Most of the people I'd met at sixth-form college found it hard to be around me now. I hurt and the only way I knew how to express it was anger. On my eighteenth, I didn't want to remember the year before. We try and forget bad times, but sometimes it's also painful to remember good ones – paradise thrown away.

Just months before – my seventeenth birthday – had been the best day of my life so far. She and I had had a beer with James, then we'd gone across the road to mine, watched TV till my parents went to sleep, then made love clumsily but wonderfully. Nothing special, everything special.

After that, things had gone wrong. We were kids and didn't know how to stay together. I wasn't ready to be happy. I didn't know the value of what I had, above all, and a million other excuses and after-the-event rationalisations.

Now I was back at James'. I'd screamed at her new man the night before that I would finish things the next day, as I knew he'd be there at the party.

I talked to my dad before coming over: "I might have to fight this evening, dad."

"Are you in some kind of trouble?"

"No." I lied. "It's just a point of principle."

"Well . . . just keep going forward."

Keep going forward . . . I wanted to tell him all about it. I wanted him to hold me and understand, to let my body give up, but we'd never had that kind of relationship. We didn't even know a language to have the conversation we needed to have. A few years later, the roles will be reversed. He will be hurting from losing my mum and we still won't know the language. It is so bloody stupid.

That evening he showed up and I showed up. Neither of us started trouble; we'd calmed down. We're not violent men.

Late at night, I was walking across the road back to mine when I saw them arm in arm. They stopped for a moment in the moonlight, perhaps concerned as to what the staggering drunk wretch under the streetlamp would do. I realised through the haze that there was nothing good I could do, and I'd done enough wrong to these friends already. I held my bottle in the air to salute them, and stumbled to bed. He had the most wonderful girl in the world and I had a bottle of cheap alcohol.

That night I didn't sleep. I'd seen a side of myself that I couldn't bear to look at. I'd also found despair, real black despair, for the first time in my life. I knew I wouldn't be getting back together with her – ever. Loss has to be met with acceptance for better and for worse. I'd never felt this bad before. Blackness isn't a colour – it's a nothing you reach at 4am when you really don't want to live.

I cried till the sun came up. The dawn looks different through tears, especially when you've been up all night and you don't want to see it.

I heard on the radio that Princess Diana had been killed in Paris that night. I went back to James' house, as people were waking up. I told people the big important news about the person they'd never met. I can only imagine how I looked, they must have thought I really liked ole lady Di. James knew the real reason I was upset and hugged me while I sobbed and cursed the world. Thanks James, I love you.

After that I was looking for wholeness. It took me some years to clean up, but I already realised addiction wasn't the solution. For a long time, I thought it was about splitting up with a girl, but it was really about disconnection more broadly. Our lack of union had become unbearable. I became a seeker. First love and first loss had opened a door.

ANTI-SOCIAL DISEMBODIMENT

We live in a badly self-regulated, disconnected time. Basically, we're lonely toddlers in Tantrum Land. Yes, me included on many days.

People buy crap that they don't need, and do shit that hurts to fill a void that can only be filled by meaning and community. We are cut off from ourselves, others and the planet; as a result, we hurt all three.

At a conference I attended recently, the speakers almost universally agreed on this, despite coming from very different backgrounds, professionally and culturally. I noticed, however, that their proposed solutions were more or less individually focused. Is the answer to this endemic disease of disconnection an individual one? An expensive therapy most can't afford, a technique you practise on your own, perhaps some new technology? Or is it something more social, more systemic and more fundamental?

What people are waking up to is that the disease we have isn't an accident; it's a set of conditions that maintain the status quo. We are not just feeling stressed; we're stressed in the sense of pressure being applied to us. Stress is a verb too. We don't just need yoga and meditation; we need social change. Applying band-aids, while someone continues to stick knives in us, is unhelpful. Yeah, we stick the knives in ourselves often, but make no mistake who benefits from the blood.

THE BODY OF PAIN

– A small town in the middle of nowhere, East Anglia, UK

I'm 6. My dad has come home drunk again. I run upstairs in our small house to avoid trouble. I cover my ears to stop hearing the shouting from below. I bury my head under my pillow and try not to cry. I clamp down my body and try not to feel. I practise this. Again. And again. I am not home.

A VICIOUS CIRCLE

Many of the horrors of the modern world are a result of numbing and can also be coped with through numbing. We numb to pain, but in doing so numb to pleasure too, and also to our internal ethical compass. We forget ourselves to forget the world, and in doing so turn off that which would drive us to make it better.

This disastrous coping strategy can be called disembodiment – a forgetting of our most fundamental nature. Many of the ways things are set up – everything from ugly cities to ugly inequality – would be intolerable if people were inhabiting themselves more fully. Not feeling helps people cope with the major and minor atrocities of life . . . and enables them to commit them. And so it goes on.

Only the courage to gently take off the armour – by daring to sense, to "lick honey off the razor blade" – can break this cycle. Embodiment as a growing field is both profoundly countercultural – a stand against the current unfeeling madness – and an already activated swing back to sensate sanity.

Courageous ones, willing to be present: I salute you and would like to call you friends.

Welcome. Home.

SOME SCARY THOUGHTS

- Many of the features of modern life are deeply numbing
- The education of our leaders, teachers and doctors is one of systematic dissociation
- A disembodied world is a psychopathic one

SOME WAYS THE BODY IS POLITICAL

- By controlling how people move, you control how they think. This can be done by telling children to sit still in school, through military poses, subtle social shaming, fashionable restrictive clothes, etc.
- Shaping bodies shapes culture. The bodies and poses presented to us are not neutral, but serve a certain way of being.

- The postures commonly promoted in the media encourage aggression in men and weakness in women (though you'll also find the reverse of this fashionably), and both are off balance. Limiting gender roles are enforced when we mimic these fashions.
- Technology forces us to bow our heads into postures of submission and depression; staring at screens makes our eyes hatefully tense.
- Bodily intuition and empathy undermine divisive ideologies (from both ends of the political spectrum) and the isolation needed for social control.
- If someone can feel their own values, they won't merely live someone else's; advertising and propaganda are most effective on the numb.
- We have had our ability to stand up for ourselves or to take up space (which are both very literal examples of embodied power) stolen.

There are many more. The term "body politics" is no accident.

DISEMBODIED SELF-ABUSE

Things that can be subtle forms of disembodied self-abuse:

- Eating and exercise habits (including seemingly healthy ones), when taken to extremes
- Overwork and busyness
- Choice of friends and intimate partners
- Not loving one's own country or culture (which are actually part of you)
- Staying poor (long-term of when given opportunities for improvement)

Self-love is a lot more than taking bubble baths.

THE BODY OF HOPE

– Leeds University Sport Centre, UK.

I'm 18. It's my first week at University. I've been drunk all this week of course, hiding my addiction in the celebrations. I've also been pleased to discover that I've coincidentally been roomed with other drug dealers. They're from Liverpool and there are all kinds of good trades and mutual education happening. Business is booming. Under the party face, however, I'm just as suicidal as I've been since thirteen years of age. I'm slim from snorting speed, my head is shaved and my eyes are hollow.

Realising the potential hazards of my employment in the big city, I decided to check out a martial arts class. I've been searching for something for years and, on some level, I realise that learning to fight could be both practical and transcendent. I have already learnt that violence is within us all, and that no matter what a nice hippie you think you are, we all have a breaking point. "Follow your bliss" is BS, follow your pain.

I walk into the sports centre – bright lights and a mundane sterile decor – no Asian exoticism here, but what I see transfixes me. Men throwing each other around with grace and ease. Black and white uniforms flowing like spinning yin-yangs. I see the discipline I so badly need. There's a sense of "rightness" in my whole body. Of coming home. Gravity feels like it's holding me, not dragging me down. I see the father figures that I won't admit to desperately wanting. I see initiation and possibility. I see a kind of hope that there's more in my body than pain, and that love and power can come together. Aikido is an odd mix of harmony and force. It looks like dancing but there's utility. There's a seriousness to it, it's not casual or ironic. It is . . . *beautiful* . . . a word I rarely dare think since Sally.

I take my shoes off and step awkwardly onto the mat, and a new world begins. For the next three years I barely miss a class. I am not a natural, but I persist. I cling to aikido like a drowning man to a raft, and it becomes my life. I do not know the word "embodiment" yet, but I start to embody something different, something that can't be found in books or advice.

NOT STOPPING

Not Stopping

I do not notice

The raging river that I'm caught in

I perpetuate my own madness, and the cruelties of my culture

My body waits patiently,

an ally ready to help

But I run on.

The daily tragedy of how I ignore her

And seek solace in cruel oblivion

Is lost on me.

MOVEMENT-PHOBIC CULTURE

We live in a movement-phobic society. Culturally, we're shackled and straight-jacketed. Most people spend most of the day sitting still, and any kind of free movement outside of prescribed places is taboo. The idea of special spaces, like gyms, being reserved for us to move in, is actually quite bizarre.

You don't think there's a movement taboo? Try practising yoga at an airport, doing pull-ups on a train, or start dancing in the street. I've been mocked, threatened, questioned by police and even told I should be forcibly taken to a mental institution (note "mental") – just for moving my own body in simple ways. *Just for moving my own body*. Think about that.

The other side of this is that movement is strangely attractive. Dogs run up to you, tails wagging. Kids come and play (they haven't yet been limited by this social conditioning). People stop and stare. Some take photos or want to join in.

Remember too, that movement and feeling are closely connected, so this is all about being fully alive! Many people deeply long for an embodied life. Some of these people resent anyone who appears to be living one. As you become more embodied, expect pushback, expect praise and treat these two imposters the same. Know that the cage door is actually open.

If you're reading this I'm guessing that you're longing to come home, and I welcome you.

A GREY WORLD

Alone

Thoughts can justify anything

I stare out of the head-cage

At *others.*

The mind cuts, isolates and divides

I confuse it with myself.

Believing everything that I think

Others become objects, like me.

I use them.

I try and fill the void but am always hungry

The world is just a resource

I have forgotten what I love

And I have forgotten myself.

THE FIRST PLACE TERRORISTS WIN IS IN THE BODY
(written after yet another attack)

Whatever the form, the purpose of terrorism is to produce a fight-flight state that perpetuates violence. Scared people hurt people, and hurt people hurt yet more people. This is the cycle: violence – hindbrain dominance – more violence.

This fight-flight reaction causes neocortical inhibition (you get stupid) and blocks the social engagement system (you get mean). Our lizard brains take over, we're soaked in adrenaline and cortisol, and that is not a good thing for anyone. This activation leads to black and white, "us and them" thinking, and primitive, violent, ineffective response patterns.

The ineffective bit is important; if you want to effectively "fight" terrorism and not replicate it, it's necessary to first relax, soften and open. And yes, I get it, at times like these that's the last thing I feel like doing, too. The first act of defiance towards terrorism is not to hate. The fight response is not effective for fighting anything in the modern era. I say that both as a psychologist and as a martial artist.

It could be considered heartless to talk about anything but grief at such a time, and of course, any decent person feels for victims. But times like these are also very dangerous. Angry, scared people are easily driven into the arms of those who promise safety through violence and revenge. This is how both terrorists and oppressive, war-mongering governments win in the world.

FAR FROM HOME

We may find ourselves as strangers in a strange land,
far from where we began – adrift from the body
We may find ourselves refugees, lost in thought and theory,
drowning in opinion and opposition
We may find ourselves astray in the pages of a book,
far from home, longing for the shores of animate aliveness.

DESPERATION

Today, while listening deeply to my body, I found something under the busyness and the "stress" (the socially acceptable, middle-class name for unhappiness). I found something that nobody wants to admit to, that I was feeling for myself and maybe for all of us: a "loser emotion", that not even a new-age type who pretends to be vulnerable to get laid would admit to: DESPERATION.

Under it all, under the confidence, the having my shit together and the pretending to have my shit together for marketing purposes, the soft animal of my body is desperate for me to listen to her. She's dying like the planet perhaps, and certainly running blindly towards a wall of doing, certainly being eaten by a cancer that few dare to admit to.

I'll see all you somacide deniers in hell, because if we were brave enough to really be honest, we'd admit part of us all is already there, and we have nobody else to blame.

This isn't a cry for help; this is a confession and an accusation. I'm actually doing great; I'm feeling strong enough to go there, so worry about yourself and not me. We are all, deep down, as fucking desperate as the fingertips of a drowning man – all that remains above the darkest ocean of despair – as he still smiles in the depths.

COMING BACK

Sometimes when I come back to my body and breath, I feel so sad.

I whisper, "I've missed you darling. I'm so sorry to ignore you.

Thank you so much for still being here, my lover,

I'll never abandon you again"

And we embrace and it's beautiful

And she holds and heals me

Like no other .

And then I break my promise. Every. Single. Time.

It's heart-breaking,

And

She always forgives me,

And always takes me back.

AN INITIAL PRACTICE

Before we get too far into the book, I want to give readers a useful tool. Embodiment is nothing if not a practical field, so here's a brief centring practice. "Centring" is a broad category of techniques used for self-regulation – for getting your shit together under pressure. Students regularly tell me these are some of the best "quick wins" from embodied learning. If you have any kind of stress in your life, they're really useful. I've written a whole e-book on this subject, but here are a couple of classic techniques.

The basics

First, think of something stressful in your life. Nothing too hardcore or traumatic, but something a bit annoying or anxiety-provoking. After a few seconds, notice what you do in your body. Very likely it will be some kind of tension or collapse. Now, stop doing this. Simple. You just learnt to identify and reduce your distress response. Physiological distress responses are not useful as they make us less healthy, less smart, less creative and less kind.

Often, it's useful for people to have a set technique to practise, to use when they know they have a stressful event coming up, to get them into a better state. Such an event could be a job interview, a first date, a presentation, or putting a child to bed. Try this ABC technique now and notice how is impacts you. If it seems helpful, practise it for when you need it. With practice, it should only take a few seconds to do. It should be done with the eyes open so you can use it in any circumstance.

ABC Centring

Aware – Be aware of your body sensations here and now. Feel.

Balance – Bring your physical body into as balanced a position as possible, and balance your awareness all around you.

Core-relaxation – Relax your eyes, mouth, throat, chest and belly.

Notice if you feel different from before you centred.

You could also add:

Connect – Think of someone who makes you smile. Connect with those around you.

See my e-book, "Centring" (https://embodiedfacilitator.com/product/centring-why-mindfulness-alone-isnt-enough-e-book/), for more on this topic, as well as later chapters.

CHAPTER 2

WHAT IS EMBODIMENT?

There's no one answer to what embodiment is. In workshops and interviews, I've found that it's useful to describe embodiment in a number of ways – some technical and rigorous, some experiential, and others more poetic – and then to clear up common confusions. So that's what I'll do in this chapter.

AN EXPERIENTIAL DEFINITION OF EMBODIMENT

Notice your arm. Approach it as an object, a thing, not you. Poke it like you would an inanimate object. Notice how that is.

Now relate to your arm. Relate to "it" as part of you. Feel. Move. Perhaps remember how this arm has been part of your battles and loves, held babies, cooked meals, washed clothes, created art, and been part of your life. Feel and move. Notice how this is. This is embodiment.

SOME SHORT DEFINITIONS OF EMBODIMENT

- How we are
- The manner of our inter-relational being (how we are)
- The subjective aspect of the body
- An ontological[4] approach to the body
- The body as "I" not "it"
- A type of intelligence

---

4 The philosophy of being.

- A view of the body as more than meat, more than a thing, and more than just a "brain taxi"[5]
- The overall umbrella term for body-mind disciplines such as martial arts, yoga, bodywork, improvisation and conscious dance
- The body as a verb, not as a noun
- Being most fully alive, and most simply human
- The magic of the ordinary
- The art of coming home
- Not what you think![6]

THE DIFFERENCE BETWEEN THE BODY, MINDFULNESS AND EMBODIMENT

Any potentially embodied discipline, such as yoga for example, can be done in three ways:

- As exercise (the mechanical body)
- As a body awareness practice (being aware *of* a body)
- As a self-awareness and development practice (being aware *as* a body)

While this book is clearly making a case for embodiment (i.e. being aware *as* a body), I am also not against simple exercise or mindfulness.

SOME TERMS RELATED TO EMBODIMENT

Somatics

I want to briefly mention the term "somatics", as it's probably the most common term used interchangeably with "embodiment". Somatics is an old Greek word and now is used to refer to the body in its lived social, emotional, political, spiritual wholeness. Often, somatics is associated with bodywork, healing and movement arts, where the emphasis is on internal experience. While it can be used as a synonym

---

5 Credit to embodiment teacher and author Francis Briers for the term "brain taxi".
6 Credit to the BMC KLC community in North Carolina for the one.

for embodiment, it can also refer to a loose grouping of Wes
ness practices, such as Feldenkrais and experiential anato
the wider field of embodiment.[7] As with embodiment, there
agreed definition, but when working through this section of
you may get a sense of differences between the two terms.
avoid the term somatics, as I find it's unfamiliar and a turn-off tᴗ ɪɴany,
and the word embodiment more accessible as an already existing,
commonly used English word.

Bodymind & bodyfulness

The terms "bodymind" and "mindbody" are also sometimes used
synonymously with embodiment, as is "bodyfulness". "Bodyfulness"
seems to have been coined by myself, embodiment teacher Christine
Caldwell, and others; independently of one another, at about the
same time. Interestingly, the Pali term usually translated into English
as "mindfulness" can also be translated as "remembrance" with the
association of returning home or "mind-body-heartfulness". Sadly
though, in line with the West's cognitive bias, the term "mindfulness"
has become the norm.[8]

The difference between body language and embodiment

There are certain postures, ways of moving and patterns of attention,
breath and sound that correspond to various emotions, perceptions,
cognitions, actions, cultures and relationships. Embodiment is not just
about the body expressing these (we could call this body language), but
it's about the body constructing them too. In other words, embodiment
is about a bi-directional link where the body both demonstrates and
creates our being. This means that we can use postures, movements
and patterns deliberately and constructively (as opposed to historically and destructively) to better match our aims and our values. This
is embodied training. Simple.

---

7 Somatics also somewhat confusingly refers to a specific school of therapeutic
  bodywork developed by Thomas Hanna.
8 See the appendix on mindfulness for more on this.

To give an example, I took up aikido to develop a more disciplined and determined embodiment. By sitting, moving, breathing and interacting in a set way, I developed my character – in a way that mere words would not have managed. I consciously practised being different from my habits, to become different. Now, 22 years later, even though I rarely practise aikido now, I look and feel like a martial artist; and have the benefits (and the risks) that this brings, as I have been changed by the practise.

STATE VS. TRAIT, CONSCIOUS VS. UNCONSCIOUS

Embodiment may refer to both a temporary state (e.g. "I'm really in my body now") and a longer-term trait (e.g. "He embodies kindness"). We are all unconsciously embodied, meaning we have a certain semi-permanent set of habits kept in place by our bodily being, which are our traits (or patterns). However, most of us are not consciously aware of these traits or their development. For example, someone may have an unconscious aggressive embodiment of a chronically tight jaw and belly, contracted eyes, angular movement pattern . . . but really has no idea, as it will just feel normal to him. We can all lose touch with ourselves (our state), but we are never fully disembodied (traits remain). We can be more or less aware (conscious of our state), and shift this if we have tools; but who we are (trait) is always underpinning this. With practice, over time, we can influence the latter too.

Embodiment can be thought of as the journey to become more consciously embodied, in both state and trait. We develop from an accident to a deliberate self-creation.

EMBODIED INTELLIGENCE

Embodied intelligence is a way of thinking about embodiment as a set of concrete skills. Combining Daniel Goleman's model of emotional intelligence, my own maxim of "awareness and choice", and working with both state and trait; we have the model below. On the left of the box we have self, on the right other; on the top awareness, and on the bottom choice/influence. State and pattern show the short and long-term aspects of all of these as the third dimension. This may seem complex now, but each aspect of the diagram will be fleshed-out as the book progresses.

A model of embodied intelligence

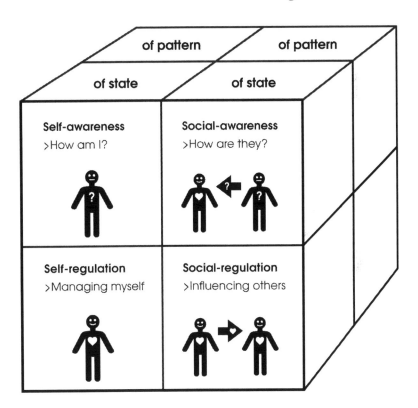

THE EDUCATIONAL BODY

– Leeds University, UK.

I'm 20. The classroom is like all the others I have spent the last 17 years in: square, dead and dull. This is the culmination of my Western education, a presentation of a psychology dissertation on another grey rainy day. I'm standing at the front of class for a change and I see my course-mates looking back, the life having been almost entirely squeezed out of their limp disowned bodies. They're a good enough bunch, they've just been taught to be in their heads since they were kids and now, apparently, we're all done and ready for the world. I jump with sarcastic joy. Not literally of course, I've been taught not to do that.

One face looks very different however, my best friend Rachel's in the front row. She's beaming, her face as ever framed by her bouncy long dark hair. She holds the happy hopeful part of us. She dances often and smiles more. Her eyes are bright and body full of vigour from all the swing, jazz dance, hugging and loving. I think she likes me in my new suit. Normally I'm scruffy, hungover and barely washed, unless it's an aikido evening, but today I thought I'd make an effort just to be contrary. It's partly because I like messing with expectations and partly because I don't want what I have to say to be ignored because of my appearance. Her smile lights me up and gives me confidence. She'll be dead from suicide in a few years, but I don't know that now. The world is not always forgiving of such sweetness.

I grin like a fox that just stole your dinner and begin my presentation on "The psychology of aikido and the meaning it has in practitioners' lives". Leeds University has a typical UK academic psychology department and talking about meaning and embodied practices is not normal here. It's taboo, in fact. People have already started to look confused. By the time I've shared some beautiful pictures, a poem, and suggested people pay attention to their posture while listening, the audience are scratching their heads like bemused robot cartoon characters. No, it's not in there . . . that's my point. The people in front of me aren't aware of their bodies – why would they be, they don't see them as relevant. As one PhD friend said to me "My body is just a cart that carries my head around." My own body right now is fizzing and buzzing with glee, as I get just a little closer to my life's purpose.

I go on to talk about the embodied learning so missing from the education system, and how people find aikido and other embodied practices so enriching as a result. I make a passionate case for how this type of knowing is needed in the world, describing the things that can go wrong when it's not present. Someone asks to see my statistics. Rachel puts her head in her hands for a moment, shakes her hair and then goes back to smiling at me. I'm giving it all that I've got and it's clearly not landing. Impassive blank gazes stare back at me like cows who have been shown a Kandinsky. It's not that these people aren't clever – they're too clever, in fact – it's that I'm speaking another language. I'm on about another kind of clever. I feel depressed, there's a smattering of applause like an emphysema sufferer's last breath and I go sit down. Rachel gives me a hug, a wet kiss on the cheek and my tense shoulders a little squeeze.

I wonder where I can go now. The job-fair last month was even worse. Just as disembodied and with values I couldn't relate to. I left in tears after speaking to people who thought they could buy my life for a wage and a pension. I'm heading off backpacking for a bit in South America, then maybe down to Brighton to see what's going on down there. I hear it's a little more alive and the aikido's good. Plenty of yoga, dance and other interesting stuff too. Maybe I'll work with kids again, I like how vibrant they are, but to be honest the future looks pretty bleak, more cerebral concrete-grey getting by . . .

"YOUR" BODY?

What do you see the body as? Something generally ignored? Or is it *your* body (as language would suggest), as if you're the controller of a puppet? There are plenty of good reasons why we may view the body in these ways, but there's a price to pay: ill health, lack of emotional intelligence, relationship issues, lack of access to intuition or the quiet voice of whispered values, and just not being fully alive. God, it's tempting. I don't want to bloody feel the pain either, but to be cut off from oneself is a slow death.

In any event, we're all unconsciously embodied, so that the body is involved in everything we do, regardless. It impacts perception, cognition, mood, relationships and ultimately the life we do or don't have. We can be half dead from the neck down, but not fully disembodied, in this sense.

We can develop body awareness as a mindfulness skill. Here, we're aware *of* the body. The body is still not us, though. It's outside ourselves, but we are at least in communication with it. The body is useful, at least, and some health and bodily intelligence returns.

And then, we can become consciously embodied. We are aware of ourselves *as* a body; the *how* of our being comes into light, and choice enters as a result. This is embodiment: the realisation that we're not separate from the body we can feel.

It's a phenomenological and ontological approach to the body, if you like long words. Or it's being fully alive, if you want to keep it simple.

FROM STATE SHIFTING TO EMBODIED CHANGE

We can change how we are in the moment (state shifting), and how we are long-term (embodied change). It is useful to be working on both of these. Note which of these a practice impacts. State shifting activities may feel good, trait building activities may not.

THE TEN LAWS OF MOVEMENT*

1. Movement is life; the dead don't move.
2. Movement is not an accident. It both expresses and creates who we are. We are human *movings*.
3. We think, feel and perceive in the same way we move. These things are impossible without movement and more so, can be changed with movement.
4. How we move is how we connect and communicate with others, and we can change this with movement.
5. Others – dead, alive and yet to be born – live in our movement. Spirit speaks to us through movement.
6. We can take action and create only through movement.
7. Powerful, beautiful and loving movement is integrated and efficient. Power, beauty and love are one way of moving.
8. Powerful and beautiful movement is free flowing, without rules – including these ones.
9. Our culture and its problems with war, the environment and social injustice are a style and stagnation of movement.
10. Our history, the present and our future moves through us; the latter can be moved.

* These also amount to a definition of embodiment.

THE BODY OF PURPOSE

– The Green Line, Nicosia, Cyprus.

I'm 25. With me are a gaggle of Arabs, Americans, Serbs, Jews and other ethnicities from warring countries around the world. I lead this unlikely group out of the once luxurious hotel, now United Nations fortress, into the last of the afternoon's sunshine. The dusty heat of the Cypriot day is settling into a serene evening. Most of the people with me I met for the first time a few hours ago and the conversation was . . . a little tense:

"I've been taught my whole life to hate you."

"I almost didn't come here, and I'm still not sure that meeting you is a good idea."

"Don't take my picture – if my neighbours knew I was here they'd kill me."

Everybody's checking each other out. We have different religions, cultures and languages and oh, most of us have trained for years to be lethal martial artists, capable of taking out a room full of people barehanded.

Walking carefully behind me are the Jordanians – making nervous jokes with some Israelis, which is a good sign. With royal panache and Queen's English, the Amman group are easy to like. Another Arab group nearby look tired but cheerful. They're earthier than the Jordanians – big, jovial and kinda square looking. They're tired because they had to drive for 48 hours before they could get a plane here: "We drove around the country that wouldn't let us in!"

The film director with us and his Greek-Cypriot camera crew pan around and catch Paul Linden right at the back. Like the director, he's small and bearded, a humble man whose right arm trembles with Parkinson's disease, but looks like he's on a relaxed county stroll. He's a master of embodied training and the Parkinson's is one of God's sicker jokes. He wise-cracked about it when I tried to ask sensitively what it was at dinner last night, "I'm here to shake things up!" He works through the body with trauma survivors, which is most of us here.

Walking out of the Ledra Palace Hotel, the British UN soldiers smile back under their sky-blue berets, with bemused, stubbled faces, but are professional as ever. They've been friendly all day, scanning us for bombs, checking passports and asking me to translate, "What your bloody Yank boss is saying?" The squaddies here are younger than me mostly, and have just come back from Iraq. None of them want to say more than a few words about it. "Difficult" was the answer when I asked an officer. The teenage privates used the words "fucking" and "horrible" when I asked them, and the aged sergeants just shrugged and looked away sadly. I can tell everyone's relieved to be here in Cyprus.

As we walk out past the sun-winking razor wire, I remember coming into the Ledra for the first time last year. I'd felt like James Bond meeting my contact and being ushered into the decaying bowels of the once luxurious UN command center. Before the '74 war, this was the fanciest hotel on the island – now it's home to several hundred British soldiers – their drying underwear and football flags draping its lavish but battle-scared balconies, redecorated with bullets and rocket-propelled grenades.

I'm not here with the UN though, but "Training Across Borders", the organisation I work for. Walking beside me now, is the project's co-founder – Donald Levine, in his seventies and an eminent professor of the University of Chicago. He'll become a mentor and see potential in me when there's little reason to now. He's talking quietly with the charismatic figure of Richard Strozzi-Heckler. It was the latter's military connections that had got us into the Ledra in the first place, I think. Don is cerebral and leads from the head, but is also an aikido sensei and gesticulates with his hands in a way which reveals his Jewish background. Richard is as composed and impressive as ever in his bearing. Philip Emminger the red-headed project manager is with them, too. Phil is a self-made millionaire, pilot and company managing-director. He's currently a hyperactive whirlwind, counting the participants that have arrived so far. I'm basically his gofer-tea-boy-bitch, which is fine. I get the impression I'm learning leadership the hard way, but at least from some great teachers. I have one luxury that the other more experienced team leaders don't have though – time. I don't know yet how many doors this event will open for me.

Now we were quite officially in the middle of nowhere. Outside the Ledra was the centre of the no man's land separating the North from the South. Called the "Green Line" after the colour that a British officer had hastily scrawled on a map in '74, it was part of a UN-policed buffer zone that ran the width of the island. It had only three crossing points and this was the main one. Cyprus – legendary isle of Aphrodite – had been torn in two, and left that way for 30 years. Philip and I had seen a young couple parting on the line a few nights ago. A Greek-Turkish Romeo and Juliet tearing asunder entwined vines of energy to go their separate ways. It was heart-breakingly beautiful.

Bouncing by my side is Tesfaye – a new friend from Ethiopia – all black muscles and white teeth. Don suggested I look after him – this being his first time in Europe. We've been sharing a room and manically making final arrangements over the last few days. It's like having a sidekick, except he's taller and better looking, which isn't the way these things should work. This Cyprus adventure is the most mind-blowing thing I've done, and for him it must be even stranger. Don's a professor of Ethiopian studies amongst other things and Tesfaye is the first East African to study aikido. Tesfaye is also part of a circus troupe that teaches HIV awareness. I'll end up living with him there for a while and having many more adventures.

All the people walking through the Green Line now practise aikido. A few are relatively new to it; many are the senior instructors in their countries. Most of the top aikido senseis in the Middle East are here – meeting for the first time on neutral ground. There are others from further afield here, too. To my left is Jose Bueno, sensei from Brazil. The aptly named "Mr. Good" in Portuguese has a polished bald head, relaxed as a Sunday morning cuddle and carries a face full of Brazilian warmth. In a couple of years, I'll be working with him, with kids in the favela slums of Brazil, experiencing much delight and getting traumatised in new and interesting ways. Jose is calling to Jamie Zimron, an American Jewish sensei and Miles Kessler. Jamie is animated and fun. Miles – along with Richard, seems the most serene – as well as an aikido instructor chiselled from years in the tough Japanese rural dojo of Iwama. He's also a meditation teacher with endless retreats in Burma under his blackbelt. We all embody our history, but it's the level of our practices that we settle to when it matters most.

Right now, I'm a shaken, stirred Molotov cocktail of emotions, enclosed in a bottle of concentrated alertness. I turn around – Jose's clicking at something – and view the whole group for the first time. I'm guiding our strange group across to the other side and it's a buzz . . . actually more than that, more like a flat sense of purpose. Of bodily "rightness" under the nerves. This is where I'm most alive, this is what I'm good at, this is where I'm meant to be. Hairs on my neck tingle and I can feel my heart pulse life, purpose and joy around my body. Between bombed out houses, where cats tread over landmines imperviously; our colourful group ambles forwards. I take a moment to beam with happiness and pride at the picture, as we approach the border.

MINDSET IS ACTUALLY BODYSET

The body is the mechanism for perception, action, emotion, relationship . . . It's also the most direct way to change these things. "Change your mind", is abstract. "Stand or move differently", is more concrete and therefore doable. "We move through space like we move through life", embodiment teacher Stuart Heller says, and the extension to this is that we can change our life through how we move, making mindset actually bodyset.

WE ARE NOT MADE OF FLESH AND BONE

We are not made of flesh and bone; we are made of love and loss.

The body is not meat; it is an autobiography.
The pieces of the body are pieces of the soul –
those that have touched us and those who have hurt us,
places we have been and people we have cared for.
The body is our values and history incarnate.
It is a sacred poem and a warm bloody world of possibility.

To know the body is to know ourselves and each other.
To be intimate with the body is to have your tongue on
the pulse of life itself.

When we cut ourselves off from the body with stagnation, technology
or addiction, we cut ourselves off not just from pain, but from joy.
Without the umbilical sensing body,
we are strangers to ourselves and others,
and violence becomes an inevitability.

My friends, I beg you, do not give up your birthright so easily.
Do not go so quickly into the numb night;
move, *move*, against the dying of your light.

*Dedicated to the people of Russia and Ukraine, and somewhat in the
style of my colleague Alexandra Vilvovskaya. And with apologies to
Dylan Thomas for the poetry theft.*

WHAT MAKES AN EMBODIED PRACTICE?

Any activity *can* be embodied, from surfing to gardening to knitting. My two criteria for a practice to be truly embodied are:

1. That it's practised with body-awareness.
2. That its aim is developing oneself.

THE ROOTS OF EMBODIMENT

We can talk about seven major influences on embodiment as a field in modern times. These fields first came together in the late 60's and early 70's in places such as Esalen in California.

Each of the seven fields is huge and complex, and too large for any individual to fully study in a lifetime. While not a complete map, they form a useful orienting list:

- Yoga and meditation
- Martial arts
- Dance (both conscious dance[9] and partner dance)
- Theatre and improvisational comedy
- Somatic psychotherapies (includes trauma modalities, dance-movement therapy and body therapy)
- Hands-on bodywork
- Western awareness arts (somatics)[10]

Some may prefer to organise this list differently. If I were to add a domain, I'd be tempted to add the arts generally as an additional one. Others could be argued for, but this is just an orienting perspective, and I'm keeping things simple here. The image below also shows that arts that may be considered embodied, may or may not be. Yoga for example, is just physical exercise in some instances.

---

9 Referring to forms of dance done with conscious awareness, as a kind of moving meditation. E.g. 5Rhythms, Movement Medicine and Open Floor.
10 Includes Feldenkrais and The Alexander Technique, which are two very influential early embodiment forms.

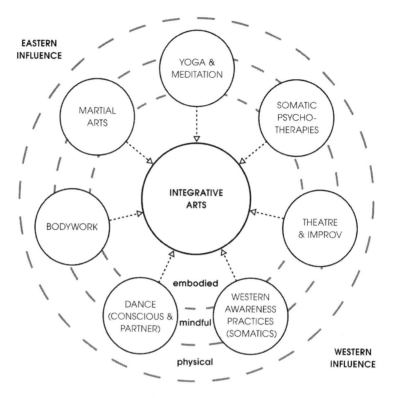

Roots of the Embodiment Field

THE SCOPE OF MODERN EMBODIED PRACTICE

Almost anything can be done as an embodied art if we define this as something done with body awareness and with a focus on developing oneself. There are however a number of established disciplines, which I've tried to map out below, and while say, 'embodied blindfold surfing' may be a thing, it's not systematised or widespread. The loose categories given can be named in different ways, relate in complex manners, and are sometimes differently titled in different places (for example "body therapy", "dance movement therapy", "dance therapy" and "somatic psychology" are not easily distinguished or categorised and regional naming differences exist[11]).

---

11 Google Kelly Mullan, who has done a PhD on this. Though we see some things differently, she's done a lot of great research on the topic, as has Martha Eddy.

The image below is an attempt to map the scope of embodied practices today, though much here is open to discussion and it is not exhaustive. Many working within this field may not know that it has an overall name, but it clearly needs one now as embodied arts both have much in common, and increasingly meet as the "movement movement" grows. I hope at least the image will illustrate something of the wonderful diversity of embodied arts that now exists and inspire you to look into some of them!

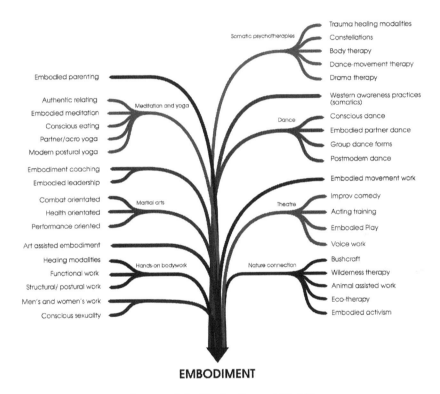

EMBODIMENT

Scope of the Embodiment Field[11]

12 Coloured larger version of this image and other images available at www. theembodimentbook.com, and a bonus chapter can also be found there.

Integrative arts and their biases

There are now integrative arts[13], as different fields collide for the first time in the postmodern context. The dialogue between these disciplines is really gearing-up today, and many of the old silos (practices in isolation) are disintegrating – e.g. it is not uncommon today for a yogi to have also had therapy or to have practised salsa dance.

Note that these arts come with particular perspectives, cultural influences and flavours. Some are more social, more verbal, more creative, more authoritarian, etc. Some are Eastern and some Western. There are things taken for granted in an aikido dojo that would be utterly weird in a dance studio, for example, and vice versa. In working with any embodiment teacher, it is worth asking where their training and therefore their bias lies, and what they are omitting. If they think they don't have a bias or that they include everything in their work, run a mile!

I encourage embodiment professionals to develop real expertise in at least two arts, to provide perspective, and reduce the negative impact of "drinking the Kool Aid". Also to gain reasonable familiarity with all seven main influences on the field, and passing knowledge of all the many sub-branches as they all bring different gifts, and will be helpful to different students. Understanding the current range and complexity available within embodiment, and helping people navigate it, is a major theme of this book.

EMBODIMENT FIELDS ORDERED BY A SCALE OF COMPLEXITY

Simple versus complex arts

I find it helpful to order the fields of embodiment training from the most simple (solo, still, non-verbal and less physically challenging) to the more complex and interactive. This is not to say the "simpler" arts

---

13 Such as Bonnie Bainbridge-Cohen's Bodymind Centring, Dylan Newcomb's Uzazu, or my own work.

are easier of course, only that the focus is narrower and the conditions deliberately less complex. The more "simple" arts (like meditation), study finer patterns and build finer skills. The challenge here is that the simple (or we could say focused) arts are most different from life, so miss out a lot. Meditation takes out much of what makes life life, for example, so there is the risk that learning is not easily transferable to daily living. Simplicity however, allows for granularity. The risk of arts involving more, is in not seeing the subtle as it's masked by challenge and complexity.

An ecology of practice

A practice reduces the complexity and consequences of life to focus on different parts of being human. If it didn't, it would be life and not a practice. By understanding the differences between the scope and "magnification" of different activities, you can see what you are learning and what you are not, and develop an "ecology of practice"[14] where you practise several arts to cover the various bases, perhaps all at once, or perhaps over time.

Note that, as things such as other people, deliberate stress, humour, sexuality and language are added into a practice, the finesse of what one may notice and may be able to control is reduced, but the ability to apply these embodiment skills to daily, noisy life, is increased.

I advise, over a lifetime at least, that people work at different points along this scale of complexity, as different skills will be built.[15] At one time, one may also want to have some "range" for maximum learning. One of these practices does not replace others, and while for most of us it's tough to do all of them at once, it's possible to cover different points on the scale (for example by doing meditation, yoga and aikido) and over a lifetime to explore all of them.

---

14 Credit to John Vervaeke for the term "ecology of practices".
15 This also relates to the embodied intelligence model previously introduced (see p.34).

A potential scale of the focus/complexity/"granularity" of different embodied practices could be*:

	Movement?	Free move/expression?	Partner?	Athletic challenge?*	Emotions key?*	Language?	Sexuality?	Consequential?
Sitting meditation	No	No	No	No	Maybe	No	No	No
Yoga	Yes	No	No	Maybe	No	No	No	No
Solo conscious dance	Yes	Yes	No	No	Yes	No	No	No
Bodywork	Yes	No	Yes	No	No	No	No	No
Partner yoga	Yes	No	Yes	No	No	No	No	No
Partner dance	Yes	Yes	Yes	No	No	No	Maybe	No
Embodied leadership	Yes	Maybe	Yes	No	Maybe	Maybe	No	No
Structured martial arts	Yes	No	Yes	Yes	No	No	No	No
Competitive/freeform martial arts	Yes	Yes	Yes	Yes	No	No	No	Maybe+
Body therapy	Yes	Yes	Yes	No	Yes	Yes	No	Maybe
Improv comedy	Yes	Yes	Yes	No	Yes	Yes	No	No
Neo-tantra	Yes	Yes	Yes	No	Yes	Yes	Yes	Maybe
Real Life	Yes	Yes	Yes	Yes	Yes	Yes	Yes	Yes

*Any practice done for a long time may become difficult e.g. meditation, however its not normal to add a intentional conscious athletic or emotional challenge - it's not integral to their design as a practice. N.b. This table is intentionally simplified for the purpose of clarity.

+ the purpose of embodied practice is to provide a safe space for people to practice in a 'dojo' where the consequences of real life, for example, losing one's job, or one's partner are unlikely.

*You could argue the position of some of these fields and of course it depends on the style of yoga or whatever, and the teacher . . . but the point is to understand that a scale exists, with finesse at one end and completeness at the other.

Note: a larger colour version of this image may be found at www.the embodimentbook.com

ALL ONE BODY

This year, I've been taking seriously a rather wild understanding: that the individual body contains everything and all of us. Yes: Everything, and all of us.

This is actually a pretty traditional, mystical/tantric notion: microcosm of the macrocosm; as above, so below; body of Christ, etc. However, it's still a pretty huge, well . . . infinite . . . idea. No . . . somatic exploration, not idea. Meditation teacher Reggie Ray pushed me over the edge with this one, but it's been nagging in my subconscious for a while.

As an embodiment teacher, the truth that the body is much more than is commonly thought, is not new to me, but the full extent of this is . . . well . . . waaayy out there. Also, I rarely speak of the deeper aspects of my work for fear of misunderstandings and creating barriers for those new to it. But the time is ripe.

It's apparent to me that I have "picked up" parts of the cultures that I've spent time in. I'm sometimes mistaken for Slavic and can boogie a little Brazilian. I have my "taking up space" American side. In Israel, there are people who don't believe that I'm not Jewish, because of how much of the culture there I can now embody.

At first, I thought this was just down to vicarious trauma and general somatic cultural influence. However, having done the trauma work and travelled so much, my sense now is that it's more that I'm accessing the "group bodies" of those places. I've danced, fought and fucked more widely than most, and despite somehow avoiding diseases that perhaps should have killed me years ago, I am surely "infected". After a while, it's all one body, and all in my body.

I've long held the somewhat disturbing view that we essentially live in one another. My old aikido teacher, William Smith Sensei, once said: "We receive each other. We become part of each other when we train together. I in you and you in me." He was dying of cancer at the time, energised by a practice with far healthier, younger men. He was not a man prone to hyperbole or esoterica.

Ancestral roots are also deeply embodied. We do the work in the body that the previous generation couldn't. We feel the grief, anger and hurt, especially. At one point, in a recent meditation, my spine felt topped by one grandfather dropping bombs (he was in a Lancaster bomber in World War II), tailed by the other grandfather in the bowels of a merchant ship that was dodging U-boats (he was a sailor), and in the middle, my heart was burning with German civilians screaming, but aided by my nurse grandmothers. Pretty intense! When fasting, I am the Irish, naturally, and also, my Ethiopian brothers. I have wept not just for many nations already this year, but *as* many nations. The ones I have kissed with lips or fists were the easiest to touch again.

Perhaps you've had strong experiences of others that you haven't seen in years? Perhaps they were more real than just memories or dreams – as if they almost have a life of their own? Vividly visiting at night? I have found this to be the case in the waking body too, with actual friends. They've picked me up from psychic battlefields as patron saints, lovers (still turning me on years later), and of course gods and archetypes (from Jesus, to Marvel heroes, to rock stars). They have a life of their own and are part of us . . . as are the politicians you despise, the homeless guy with no name, the rape victim you never met, the rapists, etc. I have given birth and flayed children alive in West Africa. I have been the babies with AIDS that I walked over on my way to breakfast, and the man who smilingly served me food at the restaurant. "Call me by my true names," as the teacher of my first love once said. Soon he will be dead. And not.

I don't often discuss such things in public. I prefer to keep my embodied work to that which I can explain with more certainty, that which is most pragmatic to people and won't scare them off. But tonight, as I reflect upon the divisiveness of the current political body, there it is. We are both sides. All sides. We contain it all. My heart beats in your chest, and yours in mine. Odd perhaps, but deeply true.

CHAPTER 3

SOME SIMPLE EMBODIMENT TECHNIQUES

Embodied practice doesn't have to be complicated or the reserve of eso-teric Eastern masters. In this chapter you can learn some of the most simple, useful techniques. Try them and see what works for you. Do not believe me.

THE MOST BASIC EMBODIMENT TECHNIQUE

Notice how you are, then choose how to be.
Work with the body to support your choice.

AWARENESS AND CHOICE AGAIN

As stated, most embodied development comes down to awareness and choice. We become aware of our body postures, how we move, stand, breathe, etc . . . and then make better choices around these actions. We then practise these new bodily actions until they become habit. This bears repeating.

BEST QUICK-WIN TOOLS

While this is not a technical book, I want to include some of the quick-win tools that I've found, over the years, to be the most effective. While different things work better for different people, there are definitely some tools that I see consistently and quickly helping most people. Here they are:

Daily check-ins

Embodied self-awareness is the foundation of all other embodiment skills, so reminders to come back home to oneself are great for anyone new to practice. You can schedule a few of these each day (e.g. using a phone alarm). Such check-ins can also be linked to daily activities such as with each toilet-break, or when making tea, and can also be integrated into larger group activities, such as meetings, where culture allows. Even a few seconds of really noticing oneself makes a big difference. The key thing is to pause, and really feel, even if briefly.

AAI

One of the simplest and best embodiment techniques is AAI. During any activity, become aware of your body, accept how you are, and then pick a clear intention for how to be. This can enhance or create a good foundation for anything, really! Once more:

- **Awareness** – feel your body
- **Acceptance** – say yes to how you are, before trying to change
- **Intention** – how would you like to be?

Walking self-coaching

A super-simple self-coaching technique is to apply awareness and choice while walking. The method is to notice how you're walking and make a choice to add a quality that would be useful. You can work with an enquiry, like, "What would a bit more ease/flow/fun/focus be like?"[16], or simply do it! This method is easy, quick, not athletic or strange, and most people have a few moments of walking daily, when they can do this.[17]

---

16 Credit to Wendy Palmer for this method.
17 Wheelchair users can apply the exact same principle, too.

Embodied gratitude

At the end of each day I like to make a short verbal or written list of a few things that I'm grateful for, that have happened that day. I do this by feeling the body fully, touching the centre of my chest as I register each item, and sometimes bowing. Research from positive psychology shows that gratitude practise has many beneficial effects, and "adding the body" supercharges it in my experience.

Make a noise!

What noise would you make right now, if you were to do so? If it's socially appropriate, go on and do it. If not, just imagine it. What does this say about how you are? What noise would be more like how you'd like to be? Again, either do it or just imagine it. A useful practice for both awareness and expression.

Embodied coin flip

If you have a decision to make, assign a choice to each side of a coin, and flip it. Not to actually make the decision, but to note how you feel about it You do not have to comply with the coin toss, but it may well give you insight.[18]

EMBODIMENT DOESN'T HAVE TO BE COMPLICATED

It can be:

- Noticing your breath a few times a day
- Leaning back onto your heels, or slowing down when rushing
- Widening your awareness when wanting more confidence
- Going for a walk in the park when stuck for ideas
- Relaxing your belly when stressed

18 Credit: Paul Linden.

SITTING AND LIFTING

Relaxation and breath are central to most embodiment systems, and while both can be explored in great depth, you can train the basics very simply. One way to do this is to notice if you hold your breath or tense up, as you sit or stand. Most people will hold their breath at some point and tense correspondingly. By breathing out gently and smoothly as you sit and stand, you can retrain habits of tension and use these simple daily acts to become more relaxed each time that you do them. Similarly, if you regularly lift things (or small people), the same principle applies. Most people tense and hold their breath even when lifting light objects, so this can become a good practice and a way of relaxing.

Simple daily practices like these can become both profound and transformative, and lead to greater embodiment benefits than doing, say, flashy yoga or athletic dance a few times a week.[19]

COMING HOME TO THE BODY CAN BE SIMPLE

Let's keep it simple. Here are ten top tips for coming home to the body:

- Spend ten minutes each morning sitting still and noticing your breath.
- Do yoga a couple of times a week. A style that's gentle and simple enough to give you space to feel is ideal.
- Eat when you're hungry and rest when you're tired (I know this one might sound idiotically simple, but trust me it's profound).
- Spend an hour a day outside in nature (a.k.a. the big body).
- Make your meetings and phone calls walking activities.
- Dance vertically and horizontally regularly.
- Take Facebook and your email off your phone; check email once a day elsewhere.
- Play with children and animals every chance you get.
- If you have addiction or trauma issues, prioritise addressing them.
- Be kind.

---

19 Credit to Systema teacher Matt Hill for this one.

SOME NON-ATHLETIC EMBODIED YOGA

Taking up space

There are a number of physical poses that have strong archetypal resonance and quickly shift how we feel. These are mapped in the Embodied Yoga Principles system and while the scope of this book does not include describing them all fully, some are very simple. One I offer to a lot of students is the Taking Up Space pose which involves stretching out the arms to the sides, above the level of the shoulder with palms forwards, and standing with the legs spread wide like a big X. It is similar to one of Amy Cuddy's famous "power poses" which have been shown to build confidence[20], and I often suggest it to students who need to work on being seen, claiming space and "owning" their success or status.

Letting go

Another excellent and easy pose is Letting Go pose, which is just a hanging forward bend. This is great for consciously choosing to let go of emotions, resentments and old beliefs that are no longer helpful. Sometimes I use it for forgiveness, or just to let go of the busyness of the day before relaxing in the evening. Breathe out, saying "aahhhhh" and relax the neck to "let the head go" when doing it.

Saying no

Hold up your hand in front of the middle of your chest with your fingers together. Do not smile and keep your head straight. Stand or sit in a stable, strong stance. This is a simplified version of No pose, and is an absolute classic for anyone who has problems saying no to themselves

---

20 Cuddy has had replication issues with proving the physiological basis of her work, but replications do show that people taking such poses both feel and are perceived as more confident.

or others, is 'too nice', or generally needs firmer boundaries. This is a great one to do if you are about to enter a situation where you might be tempted, or where someone may try and push you around. As with all poses, you can employ this as a daily practice to shift traits, and/or as an in-the-moment practice for state shifting.

Conclusion

What makes these more than physical poses is the intentionality and focus on the subjective quality of the pose. With practice, all of them can be done subtly at any time, as what we call a 'micro pose', where you trigger a practised pattern through a small movement, making them even more useful. There are instructional videos about all three of these poses, and many others from EYP, on YouTube.

THREE MORE TYPES OF CENTRING

I've already introduced ABC Centring as a pragmatic and accessible tool, but different centring techniques work for different people, so here are three more. While much can be said about state regulation, the basics are actually easy. The key thing is to try them and see what helps you in times of stress, or when you need to perform better or to connect deeper. Experimenting and practice are key, as ever. These types of centring can all be done quickly, usually with the eyes open, just pausing for a few seconds, or even "on the run". Being able to manage how you are is something of a superpower in a world where everyone is busy and stressed. Try these:

Visualisation Centring

What image would lead your embodiment in a positive direction right now? Imagining your legs as tree roots, to ground yourself? Having fluffy angel wings, to add uplift? Being made of fire, to energise? Or imagining your body as melting chocolate, to soften your state? These are just four possibilities; I'm sure you can think of more to experiment with. Use nature for inspiration, if you get stuck. Visualisation doesn't work for everyone but is a great shortcut for many.

Meaning Centring

In any situation, especially stressful ones, it's useful to breathe deeply into your body, slowly breathe out and ask yourself, "What matters here?", or, "What do I really care about now?". You can put one hand on your lower belly or heart area as you do this. Try this and note how it impacts your state.[21]

Social Centring

We co-regulate. What this means is that, as social animals, positive social connections help calm our nervous systems. A calm state can be achieved by focusing on friendly people around oneself, making gentle eye contact, or by imagining people who make us smile, even if they are not present. Just shifting attention to the basic respect between people that is usually there, to what we have in common and to how we belong can work wonders. Supportive visualisations such as of a bubble that encloses you and others, or imagining the hand of a mentor or nurturing family member on your back, can be helpful too.

---

21 Inspired by the work of Richard Strozzi Heckler.

4 ELEMENTS WHATEVERING

A simple model we use a lot on various courses is the four elements model. There are various versions of this model around (and 5 or 6 element models) but it's fairly intuitive to most people. We know for example what a "fiery" or "wishy-washy" person is like, and what we mean when we use a phrase like, "He's an airhead", or, "She has her feet on the ground".

These four elemental ways of being create a simple map of embodied preference that's very helpful as a reference point, though of course it's not about putting anyone in a box. Generally, people are good at guessing the stances, breath, movement styles, etc. that are associated with various elements, but if it does not make sense to you how each element may be embodied, you can Youtube search me teaching them, and coaching with them. This may add more detail than is intuitive as well.

While doing any activity that isn't feeling good or achieving the results you'd like, one easy technique is simply to ask yourself, "What would it be like to do this in a different elemental style?" Let's say that you are unhappily emailing, arguing with a spouse, unsuccessfully trying to get your kids to bed, or whatever; you could ask, "How would it be to do this in an earthy way?". Then in a watery way, then in a fiery way, and lastly in an airy way. Adjust your body to each of the four options. You will likely find that you were habitually doing things in one or two ways, and that the others may be more fruitful.

To offer another example, say you are giving feedback to colleagues in a "fiery" direct, passionate way that they are not appreciating. You could try a drier, more factual, slower earthier way; or a more empathic, sensitive and flowing "watery" way; or a more fun, creative and visionary "airy" way, and see which gets you a better outcome! Madness may be doing the same thing again and again and expecting different results, but without being able to make an embodied shift, this is all people CAN do! As your skill building embodied range increases, your ability to shift between elements will correspondingly.

RELATIONAL MINDFULNESS PRACTICES

Partner practice

While many people now practice sitting meditation techniques, and there is a wealth of resources available for this, few people practice relational mindfulness (being mindful with others) in a structured way. This is an issue, as often traditional mindfulness practices do not translate very well into interactions with other people, especially verbal exchanges, and people quickly fall back into habits while relating. While there can be some carry-over from solo sitting practices, frankly it's pretty poor unless you're doing A LOT of meditating, and few people have the time for this daily. This is a problem as most of what matters to most people is what happens in relationships; with friends, kids, parents, partners, colleagues, etc. To bridge the gap between solo practice and interacting freely in life – where speed, complexity and consequences mean few skills can be easily learnt – a relational mindfulness practice is essential. While some great formal relational mindfulness practices like Circling and Authentic Relating exist, these are difficult to do regularly for most, and are not yet widespread.

My solution to this bridging challenge has been to suggest students spend five minutes a day interacting with a partner or housemate very deliberately, really paying attention to listening and speaking and to their body, while doing so, and slowing the conversation right down. You could try making the first five minutes when a partner gets back from work, or before you go to bed, a time of presence. By both taking one full breath between sentences, body awareness can be maintained and habits broken. Most people find even five minutes a day like this, really listening and expressing deeply while feeling (that's the key), dramatically improves their relationships and develops embodied relational skill.

Coffee-shop practice

An alternative to this for people who live alone or don't wish to practice with partners or friends, is to make the first purchase of the day a body-aware one. Most people buy something each day from someone: a coffee, a pint of milk, cigarettes or whatever. It's possible to bring awareness to your own embodiment and to that of the person serving you and turn this into a regular daily practice. Obviously don't stare at them or creep them out, simply really look, be present, and acknowledge them as a human, not as a means to an end. Feel and look, and then feel again – that's it. You could also ask about their day and then listen and connect further. No big deal, and the real deal at the very heart of embodied practice in an objectifying world! My experience is that people really like being interacted with in such a manner, and I was even given a free coffee a few times while doing it![22]

A more challenging version of this is to look homeless people in the eye as you pass them or stop and give change, and again, feel yourself and acknowledge their humanity. This "subjectification" of oneself and of all people is the heart of embodiment.

THREE TYPES OF "ADVANCED" CENTRING

These are slightly more advanced but still relatively straightforward. Give them a try.

Choice centring

In this technique you choose between waking up or calming down your nervous system. Right now do you want to focus on deepening the in-breath to wake up, or lengthening the out-breath to relax? On bringing your attention to your feet, or to the top of your head? On extending up the spine, or on relaxing the front of your body and bending you knees slightly (if standing)? Choose what will serve you best right now. The two can be combined as well.

---

22 While usually it's essential for partners in embodied training to willingly participate, simply seeing someone as human and noticing them and yourself interacting is ethical and allowable, in my opinion!

Smooth breath

"Smoothing out" the breath so any small stops or changes of pace are eliminated is also very effective for reducing stress. Paul Linden calls this "seamless breathing" and it's a powerful technique to relax, though it requires some practice. This technique is my go-to practice for the dentist, and I haven't needed anesthetic for some years because of it.

Intuitive centring

In this technique we ask, "What part of the body would be resourcing right now?" Go with whatever "jumps out" and don't overthink it. You can then put your hand or just your attention there, and hold your awareness in this place for a few seconds. You can even ask that part of you what it has to say about the current situation, though I appreciate that this may be too kooky for some. Note, there are practices such as Focusing that go much deeper into such "body listening" methods and I teach coaching tools based upon them.

SEVEN WAYS I STAY CONNECTED TO MY BODY DURING DESK-BASED WORK

- Bookending (beginning and ending) the day with some simple yoga or other gentle embodied practice
- Stopping for a moment to notice how I feel before doing each new thing in my calendar
- Stopping work when tired (not exhausted), irrespective of what my calendar says; keeping work creative and playful, whatever it is
- Stopping to enjoy food and not using addictive eating as a way to not feel, or as a reward for overwork
- Walking in the park or around the house while taking calls
- Drinking lots of water, so I have to get up and pee regularly (timed reminders on a phone also work but are not as visceral)
- Doing a job that keeps reminding me, too (here, I'm just lucky)!

BREATH CAN BE A GOOD FRIEND

An early warning when I'm getting stupid or mean
A canary in the life-mine

An anchor when times are turbulent
A shit-getter-togetherer

A close friend. A dear intimate friend. A loyal friend
How long have we held each other, old lover?
A warm hug many times a day.
Embrace in. Embrace out.

A magnifier of passion and pleasure
Fuck yeah breath, throw my head back and turn me on,
you sexy whore

A tidal reminder of change
A reminder of vulnerability. So precious . . . and never certain.
One day you'll leave me, dear

A . . . dare I say it in this cynical world? . . .
A moving gateway to God even
LET ME BE BREATHED
I surrender. Kiss me through my veins

Breath can be a really good friend

HOW TO CHOOSE YOUR PRACTICE

Helping students pick and maintain suitable practices to develop their embodiment is quite a big part of what I do. In a world of choices, ways of picking are key.

Here are my top tips:

- What embodied capacity are you actually trying to develop? It all follows from this.
- Know that no single practice covers all the embodied skills that you could gain.
- Pick your focus, based upon your needs and your current preferences.
- Check out any teachers' ethics. Never work with an abusive teacher, but accept that none will be perfect either. If you can't see human flaws, RUN!
- The best practice is the one that you can practically do. Things like class schedule and the studio's distance from your house matter more than may be apparent at first.
- Fall in love with the practice. Commit to it until then or for a minimal period, e.g. 3–6 months.
- Pleasure is your friend. If it's always hard (after an initial commitment period), it's the wrong practice.
- Be careful not to only follow comfort, which will just reinforce your patterns and neuroses. If it's always easy, it's the wrong practice too. Listen to your body for that deep, intuitive "hell, yes", which isn't the same as ease.
- Short periods of practise often over time are better than a lot all at once, and then nothing.
- How you do the practice matters at least as much as what it is.
- Who you do it with also matters tremendously; community, practice culture and friendships can help or hinder.
- How the practice integrates into your life, work and primary relationships is what matters. Most practices are terrible for this integration, so you may need to add more reflection, bridging practices (linking the activity to life), micro poses (see the pieces relating to EYP) and other life transfer methods.

It's totally valid to ignore all of this and just go with gut instinct . . . just don't fool yourself.

PRACTICE CHECK-LIST

After reading this book I hope that all readers will establish a practice if they don't have one already, or reignite one that they have previously had. Here's a check-list for both reassessing something that you're doing, and for picking a new practice.

❏   I have a clear goal for the quality I'd like to build through the practice.

❏   The practice does not risk deepening my existing character flaws.

❏   The practice builds skills that I need.

❏   I have a plan to integrate learning from the practice into my life.

❏   There's evidence that the teacher and senior students have become better people through the practice.

❏   It's convenient. It fits with my life.

❏   My gut says "hell yes" to the practice. It's definitely a body wisdom yes and not conditioning.

❏   I love it, or at least can grow to.

❏   I can stay open in this practice and be surprised by it.

❏   Doing this practice will make the world a better place (and not just make me feel better). Concretely and directly.

TODAY I DECIDED TO BE HUMAN

Today I decided to be human.
I went for a walk when I had "lots to do", because busy is a choice.
I smelt the roses
and the dog shit . . . to be fair.

I watched some trashy TV
I ate what I liked and didn't feel guilty.
I grunted in yoga and didn't bother to try the "advanced" pose.

I didn't pretend to transcend my money worries
and didn't just say, "fine" when meeting people.
I got grumpy with my wife
and apologised a bit later than was ideal.

I sat with myself kindly on a park bench
and breathed.
I decided not to brutalise my body with mind-enforced deadlines.
I simply felt when was enough (food, work, sex, whatever)
and gave myself a break from self-tyranny.

Today I decided to be human.
I went for a walk, heard the birds blabber,
ate a packet of non-organic, high-fat crisps
and forgave myself,
for being
well . . .
human.

CHAPTER 4

FOUNDATIONS

This chapter covers the basics of embodiment.

AWARENESS, RANGE AND CHOICE

"All I teach is awareness and choice. Once you get that, let's all go to the pub", I often say at workshops.

Embodied education involves:

1. Building *awareness* of our states and traits
2. Building *range* so we can step into different modes and build a long-term embodiment
3. Through these, we gain *choice*

Without awareness, range and choice there is no freedom. While embodied work may look complicated, it really just comes down to this simple list.

ON PRACTICE

You know intellectual learning alone doesn't cut it. Imagine if I claimed to be a great lover because I'd read many romance novels, or suggested you're safe to ride in my car because I'd been told a lot about driving. Websites and apps don't help much let's face it. Wikipedia has not solved the world's problems. Learning about France is not the same as learning French, let alone knowing how the quality of light is in Paris, as you have your first coffee of the day there. The reason there's even a field of embodiment is that we have forgotten some really very obvious truths about what constitutes learning (e.g. reducing learning to learning *about* things).[23]

The bad news is obvious – we can't talk, read or theorise our way back into our bodies. I hope that it's also good news not to be bullshitted about this obvious truth too. After all the motivational talks, board breaking and fire walking, endless advice and air-thumping workshops, what we really need is practice. It's the only way we've become good at anything, so we know this. Anyone who has learnt to play an instrument, got good at a sport, or mastered a language knows this.

Our embodiment is what we unconsciously practise and can become something that we consciously practise too. THIS IS SIMPLE (if not easy). Let's stop kidding ourselves. Grow up and get on with it.

NB: Ginny Whitelaw, Shinzen Young and Richard Strozzi-Heckler are all excellent on embodied practice.

THE BODY OF LEARNING

– West Midlands, UK

I'm 24. He swings the aikido staff at my head. Hard. I block as I've just been taught to and don't end up in hospital.

I had to help him onto the mat ten minutes ago, and his breath smells of death. His skin is paper thin. Once I saw a section of it come off from a simple wrist grab and he used masking tape to patch it up so he could finish the class. Cancer. He should have been dead years ago, they say. I'm fit. Lithe. Strong without being bulky. My head is shaved. I'm a live-in aikido student of William Smith Shihan OBE, and the other teachers at one of the top schools in the UK. He's a classic English gentleman and has taken me in. God knows why. The people here are kind and the real lessons from Mr. Smith aren't really about locks and throws. Aikido is a "do", a path, the practice is about character above all. Frankly, I need it.

Inside, the dojo smells of sweat, a little blood and the concentration that comes with real martial arts. It's a dojo, so has a Japanese feel,

---

23 See John Vervaeke's work on ways of knowing, as well as the neuroscience of types of learning.

though outside is a poor industrial area of England and certainly not The Orient. Later, I'll live and train in dojos above nightclubs in Brazil, full of hot women and cold beer, on a personal growth ranch full of sensitive Californians and therapists, with academics at The University of Chicago, and even with a circus in East Africa. Eventually I'll even get to the home of aikido in Japan, while working with coaches in Tokyo. But for now I'm in England, training in a very intense way.

My fellow "*uchi deshi*" (meaning "inside the door student") Polish Pete is on the mat with me. Piotr, or just "Pete", is the only foreigner here and made of Slavic iron cables. He's far better than I am at dealing with the hardships of dojo living – washing from a bucket of cold water, never having enough food (we're dirt poor and get by on odd jobs), and of course getting beaten up 5-8 hours a day. Kasia, his childhood sweetheart, smiles and waves from the side. I'm "her favourite English boy" apparently. Pete and I clubbed together to get her an EasyJet ticket to visit. At this time, Eastern European immigration to the UK had just begun and Pete didn't speak English for the first year of our friendship. He hitch-hiked here from Poland and ate berries until he found a job. A few years later, I'd be the best man at their wedding. A few years after that, Mr. Smith would be dead, and Kasia would die horribly of cancer too. I would stand by Piotr in a small town in Poland at her funeral, as he held it together the best he could, bringing dignity to the day. Two years after, he would dance by my side at my wedding, approving of my Polish-speaking wife. Then we would know what we had been really been training for with Mr. Smith: life in all its love and loss.

Later, I'll realise that aikido isn't special . . . even if your first love always is . . . and see rich embodied learning in other martial arts, then meditation, yoga, tango, conscious dance, bodywork and more. But for now, I'm fully immersed in trying not to die. Mr. Smith stops lovingly attacking me for a moment to explain that to get any pleasure you have to give yourself fully to what you do. To commit. It's like being married, he explains, something I can't yet imagine, but he's clearly devoted to his wife. I listen with ears from the future, as I am not ready yet. He sighs, sees that I have enough breath back, and we go back to training, in a way that might look brutal, but is full of love.

THE WHAT, HOW, WHEN, WHERE, WHY AND WITH WHOM OF EMBODIED PRACTICE

To practise effectively, it is necessary to consider the *what, how, when, where, why* and *with whom* of any yoga asana, dance form, martial art or whatever. All of these factors can support or undermine a practice. They are always present and always impactful.

The what?

The form of a practice could be described as the "what". For example, the asanas (poses) of yoga, the kata (movement patterns) of a martial art or the steps of a dance. The "what" is a framework for exploring oneself.

The how?

Critically though, "how" they are done is the real essence of embodied work, and is actually a simple definition of embodiment. If you do a linear pose in a circular way, a loving meditation in a hateful way, a fierce move in a timid way, or whatever, it utterly changes the impact. *The manner matters.* The manner maketh the embodied man (or woman).

The when and the where?

The postures will be quite different when done at different times of day, times of the year and in different environments, i.e. the "when" and the "where". The same pose during morning or evening, or during mid-summer or mid-winter, is not actually the same pose. Similarly, a pose done on a mountain top, in a forest, in a cathedral or in a modern office is, again, not the same pose. This is easy to miss, if you only practise in a controlled environment like a studio, which, while seemingly neutral, is not. Nowhere is.

The why?

The "why" of a practice also matters. What is motivating your practise? What is it in service to? An asana built with purpose is not the same one as one built without. This is subtle, but significant.

The with whom?

Lastly, there is always a social context for practice. "With whom" you are doing a practice (actual or imagined) will strongly impact it. Specific relationships (such as with the teacher), whether friends or lovers are present or whether you feel like you belong to a group are all factors.

CONTEXTS OF EMBODIMENT

Take all these contexts into account to gain maximum benefit from your practice. This image includes the "where" of practice previously mentioned (environmental), as well as the "with whom" (relational). It adds the fact that we are also cultural creatures (both historically and within a context), and carry the embodied heritage of our ancestors (the intergenerational layer). Most of what this book discusses is the personal layer of embodiment, and our shared biology such as the fight-flight reaction (part of the human core).

When we see a person, or in fact feel ourselves, we are experiencing at all these "layers" at once, which is why we should be cautious jumping to any conclusions. Perhaps we are just seeing a person's bad mood that day, or how they relate to their kids, or something common to their culture, not who they are for example!

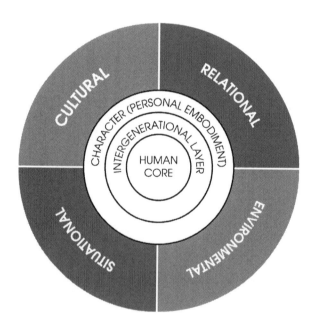

Contexts of Embodiment

CRITERIA FOR EFFECTIVE PRACTICE OF ANY EMBODIED ART

The following features should be in place for an embodied practice to make a difference:

- Dedicated: the sole purpose of the activity is to develop yourself.
- Controlled/simplified: by controlling variables, such as time and intensity, and simplifying conditions you can maximise learning and safety.
- Ritualised: this helps create a "container".
- Social (in community): we learn with and through others.
- Reflective: make time to assimilate and reflect, again to maximise learning.
- Recurrent: you need to keep doing it to make practice permanent!

We can then apply the skills of a practice in daily life, for example by being mindful during the day, as opposed to in formal sitting meditation, but do not try and replace dedicated practice with *ad hoc* application. Ad hoc application is not systematic; variables can't be controlled for ideal learning (try telling your spouse to be 20% less annoying to keep you in your sweet spot for practicing kindness for example), and consequences matter too much in real life to practise freely ("whoops, I lost my job" versus, "whoops, I fell over in tree pose").

A METHOD FOR EFFECTIVE TRANSFER OF PRACTICE "OFF THE MAT"

The previous list (criteria for effective practice of any embodied art) referred to creating a good "container" for a dedicated practice. This is vital. However, it's also useless unless such practice transfers into daily life. To put it bluntly, what's the point of having a great aikido throw or lovely yoga pose if you're a useless arsehole?

Here one method that leads to transfer to daily life:

1. Intention: have life transfer as your intention from the start.
2. Form: practise a basic posture or movement.

3. Feel: establish mindfulness.
4. Check: ask yourself whether it's familiar or longed for (shows habits and growth potential).
5. Notice: notice deviation from the "correct" form or method. You can also exaggerate "mistakes" and use contrast (this also shows habits).
6. Enquire: link to life. Ask yourself if more or less of this quality is needed in your life (or areas of your life).
7. Explore: ask what variation of this is needed (e.g. more peaceful or severe).
8. Integrate: discussion with and feedback from others is helpful.
9. Establish: practise micro poses, subtle variations of something you've been developing that you can do without looking "weird", to apply in daily life.

Adapted from Embodied Yoga Principles teacher training notes. This is just a guide and exact questions may vary. Creativity and variations are encouraged. More generally transfer is maximised by intention before, life-linking during, and reflection after a practice.

HOW TO SUSTAIN A PRACTICE

Enjoyment and discipline, are not "nice to haves" in embodied training; they're necessities for sustainability . . . and also not what most people think. If you're going to continue something to at least the tipping point of 8–12 weeks, where you'll get noticeable results, you'll need to both enjoy the process of training but not rely upon pleasure. This goes for fitness, diets, language learning, improving your sex life and other things too. Over years of training in various practices, and guiding hundreds of students on The Embodied Facilitator Course, I've also observed a series of stages that it helps to understand – somewhat loosely framed here as a romance:

1. Dating

This is the stage where you try different arts, get advice and introductions from friends, and generally "flirt" with different practices.

Stage risks: missing this stage and "moving in" too soon, or doing this forever, so not getting the benefits of further stages.

2. Initial commitment

You can't just "play the field" forever if you wish to get the real benefits from anything, you need to commit to it at some point. I'd recommend for at least three months several times a week if possible, to really get a good taste. It's best to either not start or to at least see this period out into stage 5.

Stage risks: doing this stage too early or not at all

3. The "honeymoon"

The first bit is easy, as you're motivated with a goal in mind (but don't really know what you're doing). Most people actually go too hard at this stage, due to enthusiasm, so some guidance is helpful. You don't need pleasure or discipline at this stage, which may feel like it'll last forever.

Stage risks: injury/overwhelm from enthusiasm + ignorance

4. The dip

After 3–4 weeks, life gets in the way, habits reassert themselves and the initial drive wears off. This is a danger period for quitting too soon and where three things are needed:

a) You need to remember the bigger picture of what you're doing and hold this firmly in mind. "Discipline is remembering what you love".
b) You need to find pleasure in the PROCESS, before satisfaction in outcomes is forthcoming. Enjoyment is 100% your friend and people simply never continue practices they don't like! Pleasure is a NECESSITY.
c) You need social support (e.g. a gym buddy) or a coach. We're social animals and this really helps maintain practice, especially for more

relational people. Public declarations to impose social pressure at this stage may also be helpful!

Stage risks: quitting

5. Results!

After 8–12 weeks, changes show, people start to notice and the change is more self-sustaining. If you stop before this point you've wasted your time. There are however always micro dips (plateaus and down days), so discipline and pleasure are still essential to maintain. Keep some focus here or have reminder rituals, as momentum alone is not to be relied upon.

Stage risks: premature celebration and loss of effort

6. Habit

At this stage things get easier, but . . . any practice will also have a slow, near imperceptible, but steady reduction in results, as your homeostatic mechanisms kick in, as well as reduction in motivation correspondingly over time. At this stage, there's normally a creep towards less effort and a kind of comfortable mediocrity that gradually reduces results. Usually every 5–6 months a "boost" is needed, like attending an inspiring seminar, and changes need to be made to enliven the practice and keep it fresh. You are now "married", and Friday night sex gets boring unless you mix it up.

Stage risks: stagnation

7. Identity

In time, a practice will become part of your identity. This is natural and makes it more easily sustainable, as it's not just what you do: it is you. This can take 1–2 years. At this stage the risks are losing track of why you're doing it at all and it becoming a meaningless ritual, or even not realising it's no longer the right practice for you. People can get very attached to their practices and not realise they are focusing on *the finger pointing at the moon not the moon itself*, to steal a phrase.

Stage risks: *not quitting/attachment*

8. Zen Mastery

There is a freshness and simplicity on the other side of complexity and habit. At this stage the practice itself is simply a vehicle, and becomes fully alive, spontaneous and rewarding. The danger of doing many different practices is never reaching this "deep well". Note: anyone who thinks they're at this stage, isn't ;-)[24]

---

24 Credit: George Leonard and other aikido teachers inspired some of this.

CHAPTER 5

HOPE, ENCOURAGEMENT AND HARD TRUTHS

THINGS TO REMEMBER

- You can do this
- It matters
- I love you for even trying

HOPE

I am a super "heady", ex-addict, embodiment idiot. I had depression, PTSD and still have a bad attitude, let's face it. However, I ended up benefitting deeply from embodiment, teaching it and writing this book on the topic. If I can make this journey, then so can you. There is hope.

Do not insult yourself with the cold comfort of pessimism, or enjoy the cheap pleasures of cynicism.

ANOTHER HOPEFUL THOUGHT

Empathy is bodily, not a thought. Most people who appear stupid or even evil to us, have simply lost touch with themselves, and this state is not permanent.

NEVER WASTED

No moment coming back to the body is wasted

There is no end and you've started already

You can't be bad at this

. . . And did I mention that I love you for even trying?

Please continue

YOU ALREADY KNOW THIS

It's already happening and you already know this: the "movement movement"[25] is afoot! The reason that the ideas in this book likely make sense, despite my disordered and sloppy writing, is that *you already know them*. Embodied understanding is in your bones. It's your birthright and actually it's blindingly obvious. I have made a career of reminding people, perhaps, or clarifying some small mix-ups, but make no mistake: there is *nothing* that's mine in this book. Every time you take a breath, your body knows that it knows.

As the world seems to spiral into disembodied madness, we also see a powerful return to feel reemerged. It's easy to call mindfulness apps or commercial yoga classes shallow, and there are indeed risks in what could be gateways becoming travesties. However, the popularity of these things point to the beginning of the end for the cognocentric, hyper-cerebral world view. The re-enchanting, re-embodying of the world has already begun . . . and may even be inevitable. Embodiment is a birthright that is reemerging, sometimes clumsily or even painfully yes, but being reborn none the less. The revolution has started.

A VISION OF AN EMBODIED WORLD

I can imagine a world where bodymind or embodiment education is a normal part of growing up, where embodied systems such as yoga, martial arts, meditation, trauma release . . . are taught as standard in schools, and everyone has access to the benefits of them. A world where everyone, not just an elite who can decode the jargon and afford the fees, is able to return home to their bodies. I can imagine a world where doctors prescribe yoga and nature connection, where teachers meditate daily with children, and where businesses have their own dojos. Actually, I can easily imagine all these things, as they are already happening, in some places, at least.

---

25 Credit to yoga teacher, Gary Carter, for predating my use of the term "movement movement".

Do not allow this to seem strange. Remember that once, most people couldn't read and write, except for an elite caste. Now most can. Today, most people aren't yet somatically "literate", but this need not be the case. Dare to envision a world where embodiment is not exceptional, where the extraordinary has become commonplace, where our special tools are taught as basic foundations for living.

An embodied world would be a much better world for reasons that I hope are becoming clear. I imagine this world because it's possible and because I'm feeling low today and need to perhaps. There are many things the world needs, and there is no one solution to the challenges that we face, but I know that a reunion with the body is part of a healthier picture. It feels worth dedicating myself to. When I imagine the IMPOSSIBILITY of war for deeply feeling people, or the IMPOSSIBILITY of child abuse for the empathic, or the IMPOSSIBILITY of environmental destruction for the connected . . . well, then I smile and get back to work.

EMBODIMENT IS CLOSE AT HAND

In an aikido class just across town, the sensei whom I've known for fifteen-plus years was teaching about "centre". His teachings were closely aligned with those I recently witnessed at an exotically packaged retreat in the Colorado mountains halfway across the world. The irony struck me of running around the planet to be told the same stuff as by my old friend up the road past the fish and chip shop. The local aikido was far more accessible than any I found in Tokyo, too, albeit in somewhat less appealing surroundings and without the sexy foreign trappings. But the basics of breath, posture, movement and listening are always enchanting.

I don't listen to my local teacher, and pack my bags again for another trip.

I rarely make it to the classes of some of Brighton's world class yoga teachers, one of whom is literally teaching in the next street along. And they all have quite small groups here. Similarly, I myself attract far bigger crowds of students in Moscow than in London, and my colleague Vilya from there is given an exotic status here! "Prophets have no honour in their hometowns", and all that. What does this mean for the home of embodiment I wonder?

Taking this deeper: embodiment, of course, is the most obvious and most literally "at hand" thing there is. We're running around manically looking for our jugular veins! We're taking hundreds of exotic, distracting new lovers, not realising that it's our wife of deep self that we really love. Trying to find "out there" what's "in here", trying to solve an inner problem with an external solution (close to a definition of addiction by the way). We're all a bit foolish aren't we? Maybe it's time to just smile, breathe, hug the wife, and do the class in my own home.

HOW EMBODIMENT HAS ENRICHED MY LIFE PERSONALLY

Writing about embodiment can seem abstract, so this piece is about the more personal benefits of embodied training, just from my own personal perspective. This work has brought massive benefits to my own life over twenty+ years. Likewise, I often hear positive things from my students that aren't related to their professional learnings. For example, recently a Norwegian student told me that the Embodied Facilitator Course (EFC) saved his marriage.

Here are some of the ways embodied training has enriched my own life outside of the professional context in which I use it daily:

Trauma and addiction recovery

I might as well dive in at the deep-end. Embodiment from my first explorations of the martial art of aikido to the present day has been a journey of healing. Embodied practices has helped me overcome trauma and has been an integral part of my sobriety journey over the years. For example, the self-regulation skills of centring are very, very useful when this ability is damaged from trauma and addiction.

Learning how to rest

Self-care did not come easily to me, but embodied practice has taught me a kinder, gentler way of treating myself. While I still burn brightly, I can now take rest and enjoy my life all the more as a result! I see many students take this journey too, as pushing too hard seems a sickness of our times.

Intimacy

Embodiment helps us connect, first to ourselves and as a result we can connect more deeply with others. I'm sure the profundity of my intimate relationships and friendships has been hugely enhanced by embodied training. Honestly, I couldn't imagine being married without it.

Finding purpose

Staying true to my values and deeper "calling" has been a result of tuning into myself through these practices. With students, I also see people align to what really matters to them through the body. The ways purpose enhances one's life are huge, and this impacts on many of the other areas mentioned.

Helping me run a business

Embodiment not only is my business, but it also helps me run that business. From skills around staying motivated and focused, to managing stress levels, to uses in marketing and sales, embodiment is a huge business help.

Makes me sexier

There's no doubt about it, getting in your body makes you sexier (if not modest). I joke to students that this is an unpleasant side effect of practices and often hear things like, "My wife likes what this course is doing to me".

Immunity to consumerism

We live in wonderful, but also sick times. Coming back home to the body gives a certain immunity to the madness of disconnection and consumerism that drives the modern world. Embodiment is a radical act that is also deeply linked to my politics and social change activities outside of paid work.

For the hard times

To paraphrase the late great Zen teacher Michael Stone, "Practise today, as you literally have no idea how life will call on you to serve tomorrow." I have certainly found that when the shit really hit the fan in my family (for example, my niece being born with a life-threatening condition, or when giving the eulogy at my father's funeral), I was bloody glad I had embodied practices to support me. During the challenge of managing an extended, painful forced separation from my Ukrainian wife due to visa issues, I was glad I could both cry fully and get my shit together for the next call with our lawyer.

Great friends

The greatest gift embodiment has given me is not work superpowers or kick-arse resilience; it's the people it has put me into community with. We see this on the Embodied Facilitator Course, and it's something people are often pleasantly surprised by. Embodied training has given me life-long friends, amazing colleagues I don't mind working with for 14 hours a day; and of course the beautiful, wise wife who started as my interpreter in Ukraine (with whom I am now happily living in the UK).

THE BODY CAN REMIND US OF A FEW IMPORTANT THINGS

- What we actually care about
- That we're not alone
- That we love
- That we're part of nature
- Of God
- And through all that . . . that we're alive and that we're not things.

THE PRACTICE PARADOX

There is nothing to get right and nothing to do. *And* if you don't practise, you won't get anywhere with this.

A good response to this paradox is to smile and get your mat/cushion out, then to smile again at your audacity.

THE HERO'S JOURNEY

The hero's journey of the modern age is prioritising feeling, learning and self-care over escapism and addiction. Nobody "has time" for meditation, nature, reading or yoga. The heroic make time; they prioritise, sacrifice and stay up late / get up early. That's it. If you want easy solutions, look elsewhere.

SIMPLE, NOT EASY

The good news is that embodied practice is simple; the bad news is that it's not easy. I think you actually know both of these facts in your bones, though. If not, wait until the quick fixes and weekend workshops have failed you, then come back to practise[26].

---

26 Count the number of times the word "practice" (noun) / "practise" (verb) is used in this book to understand its importance for embodiment!

RADICAL SOMATIC RESPONSIBILITY

You're mostly your fault. Admit it.

When people complain about their bodies and emotions, they tend to miss the central fact: true accidents aside, they're usually the cause of what they're complaining about!

When someone says: "I have a bad neck" for example, what they actually mean is "I bad my neck". It was their use that caused the problem – at least, the majority of the time. Sure, there may have been less direct causes, like them learning a movement pattern from society or whatever, but they still moved their neck that way.

Emotions are also bodily actions that we do, as my teacher Paul Linden has pointed out. You didn't get angry as a passive victim of circumstance. You *do* anger in the body. Emotions are unconscious choices, but choices, nonetheless. People getting offended is another example of this. No, you *did* offended, and that doesn't buy you any rights.

This is critical, because until responsibility is placed back firmly where it belongs, no change is possible. We must first admit that we alone are doing something. Only then are we in a position to stop it and choose another way.

A new definition of kindness

A radical insistence on responsibility need not be without heart. It doesn't require a moral tone, and less direct causes can also be considered. Likewise, it doesn't absolve us of kindness as a moral imperative. It is not victim blaming. Our own behaviour and the society we create are important conditions surrounding the inner somatic choices people make.

A new definition of kindness might include creating the best possible conditions for people to acknowledge their own responsibility. Increasingly, I come across victim creation and even celebration, often as part of politically correct dogma. This is one of the most vicious things a person can do, because it robs people of the possibility of change. Real kindness looks at people straight and says: "How can I help you change what you're doing?"

Feel free to be triggered. That's you, too.

CHAPTER 6

SOME SPECIFIC APPLICATIONS

Embodied training can be applied to anything, as "wherever we go, there we are"[31]. The body is always present, always involved, and therefore embodiment is useful in <u>all</u> contexts. I have applied the work to everything from corporate team building to resilience training in war zones. Aside from my "bread and butter" work with coaches and yogis, I have worked with street-kids, politicians, senior police officers, lawyers, bankers, soldiers, TV stars, tech geeks, angry chefs, abuse survivors, single mums, opera house wig makers . . . I could go on! Actually, I always take jobs with novel groups just to check embodiment can help all kinds of people, but I'm running out of new groups these days! I'm also aware that much of this little book could seem a bit abstract, so here are some examples of specific applications of the work to help you. Browse whichever are relevant to you personally and skip the rest. Feel free to share them widely, especially the sections on peace and trauma which I sincerely hope spread to become common knowledge as soon as possible, for all our sakes.

---

31 I'm not sure of the origin of this phrase, though it was used as a mindfulness book title by Jon Kabat-Zinn. It sums up the inescapable nature of embodiment nicely, though.

HOW TO FIND YOUR LIFE PURPOSE THROUGH THE BODY

One thing I've coached quite a lot of people on, is finding work that they love. Increasingly, people are not willing to do meaningless labour, unless they have to. Seeking a sense of purpose through work is now common. Because our values, strengths and deep drives are all embodied, it is of course useful to access the body when trying to deepen a sense of purpose.

Here are a few tips for this:

- Notice what lights you up. What gives you energy when you're tired? What you can easily get out of bed for? What do you have an aligned, felt sense of *rightness* when doing? Your body is your purpose radar. This may just be a small *bright spot* part of your day. Experiment if you have no idea.
- Notice what gives you that tired but deeply satisfied feeling at the end of the day.
- Notice who inspires you and who you are drawn to. Do not out-source purpose through idealisation.
- Notice what work reduces your addictions and benefits your most meaningful relationships.
- Give up all entertainment for a week in order to tune into what you really want.
- Make the posture in your body that embodies a strength – for example being open or standing firm (ask people if you don't know your virtues). What does this suggest about work you would be ide-ally suited for? Try with several strengths.
- Notice what breaks your heart right open.
- Simply ask your body what you're here for. Go into the wilderness without distraction and wait for your body to speak. Meditate deeply on the question, "What am I here for?" Be patient.
- Face your inevitable death. You can, for example, meditate on the eventual disintegration of your body (try searching for my "Death Meditation" on my YouTube channel).

See the "Purpose Black Belt" videos on my YouTube channel for more on this subject.

RESILIENCE TOOLS FOR TROUBLED TIMES

Here are some tips on keeping your head amidst the insanity of the world today. Well, more like keeping your body, as those around "lose theirs and blame it on you", to misquote Kipling. Resilience is the ability to bounce, rather than break under pressure, and we all need this.

Everything below has been tried and tested in areas of conflict, in martial arts dojos, in stressful workplaces, and with activist groups on global frontlines. Embodied resilience is a specialism I developed first as a humanitarian worker and then through teaching others in the most extreme environments. These days, I joke that even an average office feels like a war zone, and the political climate certainly does, so we can all benefit from these tools.

Resilience is about three embodied reconnections:

- to self
- to others
- and to something bigger than oneself

Put your own oxygen mask on first

This is a bit of a cliché in personal growth now, but it's still true: we need to look after ourselves first to help others. Diet, exercise, sleep . . . are and always will be the basics of being a healthy human being; that's our foundation for action. Self-care and self-love are often under-developed in those trying to change the world, in my experience, so watch out for this one!

Connect to yourself

While it's tempting to avoid feeling when unpleasant emotions abound, we can only stay healthy, compassionate and effective if we're in touch with ourselves. The first connection is to come home to the body. This is the basis of many of the skills people need during tough times, and it takes practice in our disembodied culture. Body awareness meditations, gentle yoga, massage, tai chi, and many other practices can be helpful.

Get yourself together

The completely natural and totally unhelpful response to pressure is the famous "fight-flight-freeze" (FFF) response. This is where most of the world seems to be at now, but it's a problem if we wish to constructively engage. The reason FFF is an issue is that it's:

- Self-destructive: it's exhausting and makes us sick if it's a longer-term state.
- Capacity reducing: as the hind-brain 'hijacks' us, we lose intelligence, compassion and creativity. FFF makes us stupid and mean.
- Not compelling to others: if we want to be persuasive, hate isn't helpful; it simply puts others into a defensive pattern of their own, and the destructive cycle continues.

So, what can we do? Well, love *is* the answer, not in an abstract, hippie way, but as a practical, embodied tool, using posture, breathing and awareness. Martial artists, who have learnt the hard way, call the methods for reducing the FFF response "centring". These methods are vital during tough times.

> *A very simple one you can do right now is to feel your body, stand or sit in a more upright and balanced way, and relax your eyes, mouth and belly. Notice the difference.*

Embody your stand and hold your "no"

There are several, often underdeveloped, embodied capacities that can be deepened as the Molotov shit-filled cocktail hits the fan. Two of these are being able to make a stand and being able to say a firm, non-violent "no". These are good antidotes to the natural "flight" response we may feel when faced with pressure. Search "**No Pose**" on my YouTube channel for a posture to help with this[32], or simply practise standing your ground while imagining whatever the threatening thing is coming towards you. Calibrate what you imagine, starting small and working up, so that you are not overwhelmed. Having a friend place a hand on your back can also be great for tuning into a somatic sense of support. When they are no longer there you can simply imagine it.

Do the healing work

Times like these can bring up a lot of old traumas and shadow (e.g. in our relationship to power or authority). For us to be at our best, it's necessary to heal where we can, so as not to be trapped in cycles of violence. Hurt people hurt people, and this applies to us too. A positive frame here is that now we may be forced to do the inner work that we've needed to do for years!

Connect to others

We are inter-resilient. We care for ourselves, heal and fight oppression most effectively in community. You're only as resilient as your social support. Building supportive networks and reaching out to them is vital. Learn to listen, learn to ask for help, learn to express yourself. Learn to give and receive appreciation. Get the hugs in. Eat together. Laugh at all the bullshit. Dance. Connect. You get the idea.

Here's one little trick for when you're alone and feeling rough:

Imagine the hand of someone who has supported you on your back. It feels good, right? You can also look for what you have in common with those around you, even if they're not particularly friendly. Look for what you like about them, even if it's not much.

---

32 demo'd by Daria Walsh for those who are curious by the way.

Connect to purpose and values

It's easy to lose track of what you care about when things are stressful, yet keeping this connection brings us strength. At any moment, just asking "What do I care about?" or "What am I in service to" can be very helpful.

Putting a hand on your heart, womb or belly can help with this.

Also, we all have something bigger than ourselves that "has our back". Sometimes this is a sense of where we come from, nature, an abstract idea (like truth), or a religious belief. Tuning to a felt sense of this connection when you have it can help you access it when you need it.

Anger is your friend, hate isn't

Anger has been demonised in the personal growth scene, at least in more "new age" circles, which is a pity as it is simply passionate caring (as Zen master Junpo Kelly points out). Off balance hate on the other isn't helpful for the reasons already outlined, and while it may be tempting to use it as a "fuel" as it does energise, there is a cost to this personally and relationally. Staying away from both anaesthetised fake calm, and out of control rage, while not fearing fierceness, is a fine and necessary art to learn. There is a reason warrior pose is part of the yoga repertoire.

Learn to play

The opposite of stress is play. Keeping a sense of humour, accessing creativity, and being playful – even when times are tough – is vital. When I work with people and they lose this, burnout is often approaching. Equally, play has a particular embodiment (that we all know, even if out of practise) and we can tune into it this way.

Say thank you

In times of anger and uncertainty, it's even more important to practise gratitude for what we do have. This fuels the effort required to change what we want to.

> *Practising gratitude verbally, with gestures (bowing is great, for example) or in writing, is one of the most reliable and effective ways to manage mood, in my experience. Make it a regular practice.*

Conclusion

Different things work for different people and it's good to have a diverse bag of quick-win tools, but also to look at deeper patterns around things such as boundaries and self-sacrifice. Enjoy!

BEING SEXY

We all know someone who doesn't look like a magazine model, but is confidently rooted in themselves, and as a result seriously sexy. Or we have a friend who's open, empathic and drop-dead gorgeous because of it. Or maybe we know a leader who has presence, gravitas or charisma that makes them attractive in a way that transcends six-packs or makeup. Embodiment is at the heart of a deeper approach to being sexy, and actually it's far more effective than superficial means.

Embodied practice makes us sexier

We've been sold a lie about beauty being skin deep and, frankly, it's insulting. The fact that attractiveness goes beyond media distortions is perhaps obvious. The next part, however, may be new: through embodied practice you can easily reveal a way of being that makes a person authentically sexier, without compromising or pretending. The capacities involved are critical for life anyway, and they outweigh the physical factors that much of the world feels are so important.

Screw the media lies, forget the botox and the slickly marketed status symbols. Here's how you unleash "inner" beauty. It's not really about building something new, but about fully expressing how we're attractive anyway. Some might have rejected beauty entirely or say it's completely in the eye of the beholder. But let's be honest: *wide agreement does exist.* And who doesn't want to be attractive in one way or another? I appreciate this can be a painful topic, due to the pressures on women and, increasingly, men. However, it's one I constantly hear people are interested in, so better to offer an approach that may align with people's values, rather than just deny it as an area of concern.

"Embodiment" refers to relating with the body as an integral part of who we are, not to the body as an object of athleticism or surface beautification. So, obviously embodiment has a different take on beauty and attraction. What I've seen, actually, is that embodied work impacts this area strongly, even when this is in no way the focus! For example, teaching centring for stress reduction or leadership has also instantly made people lovelier. Relaxed, confident, open and connected people are attractive. Who would have figured?! What's more, I saw that long-term embodied practice made students more and more gorgeous. On EFC, our train-the-trainer course, it's quite obvious that the whole group gets generally yummier during each year, despite the fact they aren't trying to work on this at all! Similarly, I'll often coach an executive to increase confidence and he'll mention his wife's increased sexual interest. I'll be supporting someone to develop more emotional intelligence and, all of a sudden, people start asking her out. At yoga festivals, I've noticed it's common to think, "Where did all these amazing looking people come from?" by day three, when everyone has refound their bodies. And so on.

Eventually, some clients started asking me to help them specifically with attractiveness, so I developed more knowledge in this area. I feel a little vulnerable saying this as there's often push-back (people often being triggered by the pain of social pressure to look a certain way) and a "who are you to say?" vibe. I get it, I really do. It's a scary topic for us all; nobody wants standards imposed or the magic and complexity of human beauty put into boxes. Frankly, it's a risk to go here at all. However, I think an embodied approach really serves people in a non-judgmental way that provides a great alternative to the mainstream lies.

So, here are some top tips for deep attractiveness. These are all trainable with embodied practice, which is great news, and again,

I do appreciate, can be hard to hear. Of course, it's more complicated in reality, due to such things such as polarity, typology, culture, developmental level and just plain old taste . . . but still, this will be a useful starting point for many.

Presence

- The first step to an embodied approach to beauty is to get in your body. This alone makes a huge difference to how sexy you'll feel and seem. Presence is hot!
  - Practical exercise: feel your body now!
  - Long-term development practice: commit to any mindful movement practice, like yoga, conscious dance or tai chi, and practise embodied meditation.

Ethics

- Be a good person. Violence is ugly.
  - Practical exercise: wish yourself and others well. Think of someone who makes you smile inside.
  - Long term: work with a system of ethics as an ongoing awareness practice.

Confidence

- Who doesn't find confidence attractive? This is a big one.
  - Practical exercise: stand tall and "take space".
  - Long term: take up a martial art or extreme sport, where you can practise embodied courage.

Calmness

- Panic isn't attractive. Non-reactivity (balanced with play and expression) is.
  - Practical exercise: relax your jaw and belly. Breathe.

   – Long term: commit to a practice, like yoga or martial arts, that involves practising relaxing under pressure.

Radiance

- Being "radiant" or "shiny' is not magic and does not come from shampoo or makeup. It is hot.
   – Practical exercise: imagine you're a light bulb shining or a glow worm's butt radiating light (credit to my mentor Paul Linden here). Don't collapse. Extend.
   – Long term: do this exercise daily.

Empathy

- In a world that doesn't listen, someone who does is deeply attractive.
   – Practical exercise: open and soften your body. Pay full attention to someone else; listen without judgement or interruption.
   – Long term: commit to an embodied relational practice like aikido or partner dance; or a more literal embodied relating practice like Circling.

Depth

- People who've loved, lost and really experienced life deeply are more attractive than those who've lived on the surface.
   – Practical exercise: ask yourself what you care about right now. What matters?
   – Long term: face your death and find your purpose. Love fully.

Playfulness and emotional expression

- Being embodied is expressive and playful. It isn't all about self-control and becoming centring robots. When we say someone is "fully alive", this is what we mean. And guess what? It's hot.

- Practical exercise: go dancing, shake your arse, let it all hang loose, scream, shout and cry. Hang out with kids more.
- Long term: take up improvisational comedy.

Conclusion

There are many more I could add here. I haven't talked about fierceness or gratitude here for example. Hopefully there's enough here to help kickstart things. Beauty – or attraction specifically – is a really big part of life that can bring a lot of benefits for us, our loved ones and the world. I wish you well unleashing it further, should you wish to.

NB: See the "Beauty Black Belt" videos on my YouTube channel for more on this from me and Mrs Walsh.

---

19 TIPS FOR TEENAGE BOYS AND YOUNG MEN

My sense is that there's a need to better support young men into maturity. I have worked with about 20,000 boys and teens in fifteen countries, so have some relevant experience. Here are some places to start if you're a young man or wish to pass this along to one. While I have worked with a similar number, I feel less qualified to talk about girls and young women, as personal experience is so key (so I have asked my colleague Jane Dancey to cover this area). Some may ask why I don't just offer advice to all young people, and much of what is said below is useful to any gender, however, in every culture in human history I've studied, men and women have been supported differently in their maturation and I don't believe that this has been an error. So, at the risk of offending someone in these politically correct times, here are my top tips for boys and young men:

- Check the qualifications of anyone offering you advice. Are they happy, healthy, wealthy and loved? If not, ignore them. Look at their actions and their relationships. Listen to successful older men, by whatever definition of that you have.

- Develop your character. This is the main subject of this list. Skills can be learnt, situations and technology change, but you are always there – at the scene of the crime. Who you are is a work-in-progress.
- Learn to fight. You're useless to your loved ones if you can't protect them, and the personal growth from a martial art can't be found in school. Become strong across as many domains as you can. Do not confuse weakness and compassion. Being a bully is weak.
- Honour. Your. Word. No excuses. You're the person most responsible for your life. By 30 your life will be mostly a result of your choices. At 40 even your face will be.
- You will suffer. Smile anyway. Only the weak pray for an easy life and if they get it, it makes them weaker.
- Play with kids and animals every chance you get. They are a better judge of character than you are, and will keep you vibrant.
- Learn to dance. Take one dance class for every book you read and set of weights you lift. Get into your body. Learn to both express and regulate yourself through the body.
- Know how to think well, talk well and dress well – in that order of importance. Don't make these your main aim.
- Learn how to be alone. You can't be with anyone else, let alone help anyone else until you can do this.
- Don't worry about what you're doing with your life until your late twenties. Up until then, just get drunk with interesting people, do fun jobs, pursue your hobbies fully, live abroad and learn another language (don't just "travel"), sleep around if so inclined, take some drugs (but don't let them take you), climb mountains, take risks. After thirty, start worrying about your health and learn to make money from what's meaningful to you.
- Don't apologise unless you really mean it. Speak the truth, no matter if your voice shakes. By speaking the truth, you will make and lose the right friends. Spend time in silence. Give thanks.
- With a few exceptions that only you choose, know that other people's opinions of you are not any of your concern.
- Love your mum and know that if you're older than 12, she can't help you be a man. She may try and that's noble, and she's likely doing the very best she can and should be honoured of that, but part of her wants you to remain a little boy. She may well hate the fact that she can't help you to be what she is not, and that doesn't

matter. Don't try and replace her with the first girl/boy you meet. No partner can give your life meaning.

- Come to terms with your dad, even if he's an arsehole. He's a part of you, like it or not.
- Do not try and understand women. But do listen deeply to them. Nothing will teach you more about yourself. And sometimes, ignore everything they say (including their responses to this piece), but never what they do. Pay attention to what women are really attracted to (again, not what they say they are). It's your job to try, and her job to choose. Don't feel bad for the former and respect the latter impeccably. Use poetry, humour and condoms. Always pay, if she sincerely offers to pay; don't pay if she doesn't offer to. A gentleman always offers to go down first. If you're gay, this all still applies. Being gay does not make you *any* less of a man.
- Be loyal to your friends; let go of those who do not keep this same rule. The quality of your life will be partly defined by the quality of your boundaries on bullshit.
- Devote yourself to the work and those that you love. Be useful. All the rest is babble. Tend to one's own garden; that's the proper area of concern. Seek the meaningful life; happiness and success will very likely follow.
- Know that all advice is bullshit.
- Learn all this the hard way.

---

15 TIPS FOR TEENAGE GIRLS AND YOUNG WOMEN

– from my colleague Jane Dancey who does embodied work with this group

- Know that you are enough just as you are. If you're feeling the need to be more or less than you are, that's highlighting an imbalance in the situation or relationship. If this is a recurring theme find some-one to talk this through – someone wise and clued-up or a therapist.
- Make friends with your body, all of it. Notice the parts of yourself that you find unacceptable and explore this gently with self-compassion. Get professional help if it feels too much to do on your own.

- Find a mentor, or two. Wise older women who have your back and give you advice and guidance when you need it. Don't be afraid of asking, us older women find it an honour to help our younger sisters. Pick mentors wisely of course, age isn't enough to confer wisdom.
- Cultivate great friendships with your fellow sisters, based on mutual admiration, support, love and fun. Drop the old paradigm of jealousy and competitiveness amongst fellow women; its disempowering.
- Stay active, move your body in ways that delight you. This will be so useful on many levels. Movement practices and exercise keep the body and mind healthy. Don't be afraid to try something new and different to what you usually do. It helps keep things fresh.
- Cultivate and trust your intuition and gut reaction. Movement and meditation practices will help with this.
- Get out in nature. It's one of the most effective ways of looking after your mental health. Get your feet on the grass!
- Take responsibility for your actions, own your misendeavours and celebrate your achievements.
- Embrace your menstrual blood and chart your cycle; it's one of the best ways to look after your physical, emotional and mental health. It's your own inner barometer of what's going on for you and it's the gateway to your power and creativity. Find your local "red tent" to get support and knowledge on this or check out the Red School (https://redschool.net/) online.
- Learn about the workings of your female sexual organs; there are some great books out there! Don't be afraid to learn about sex and intimacy; it's not knowledge that we are born with and learning about it is empowering.
- Part of that knowledge is that it can take female genitalia up to 40 minutes to get aroused. Yes 40 minutes! So it's really ok to take your time.
- Get comfortable in touching yourself before others touch you. Find out what you like by yourself first, so that you can communicate this to your lover; don't rely on telepathy!
- Explore consent. Notice how your body says yes or no. Find your strong yes and your strong no and get comfortable with using them

when you want or need to in all situations. Know that it's ALWAYS your right to say no and your privilege to say yes.

- Spend time with yourself, and if you find this difficult go gently with it. Start a meditation practice, take up journaling, knitting or other lone-time pursuits. This is part of self-discovery and is essential to mental wellbeing and maintaining good relationships with others.
- Get creative. Draw, paint, sew, bake cakes, garden . . . Being creative is not about producing masterpieces. Just enjoy the process of it rather than being attached to the outcome.

TRAUMA HEALING

The body is integral to trauma healing. In fact, it's been the failure of traditional talking therapies to address trauma, that has brought the body back to therapy generally in recent years. Coming from an alcoholic household and working in various areas of conflict, I developed a very personal interest in this subject. First to help myself and then to educate others. I have now worked with the militaries of various countries and numerous major aid agencies, and studied a number of somatic modalities related to trauma.

   This short piece is intended for the untrained reader, so professionals in the field may find it simplistic.

Trauma symptoms

Trauma symptoms can be very diverse but, concisely put, overwhelming experience can lead to:

- Being stuck in the psychological fight, flight, freeze or fold response (or some combination of FFFF). We are all familiar with this from threatening experiences or just daily life stress, but when stress is overwhelming, we can get stuck in this mode for a short while (often trauma responses fade in a few weeks) or an extended period of years.
- Being "fired up" from trauma, sometimes known as hyper-arousal, can lead to problems with sleep, concentration, anger and anxiety.

- Numbing, dissociation and disembodiment.
- Poor boundaries and other communication issues. We do not relate well when in this state.
- Intimacy and sexual issues. Trauma is toxic to close connection.
- Psychosomatic health issues: these can be very wide ranging but digestive, skin and breathing issues are all common. Chronic tension or "armouring" is also very common in the body.
- Secondary coping mechanisms, such as addictions, where people try to regulate themselves through drugs or alcohol, for example.

This list is far from exhaustive.

Trauma treatment

So what to do? Perhaps a good way into the large and delicate subject of treatment may be just to state the things that I've found useful for my own trauma healing, in no particular order. Different things work for different people, and while I've done a fair bit of research into the topic, I have a clear embodiment bias. That being said, a wide spectrum of approaches is usually helpful to heal the wide bio-psycho-social-spiritual nature of trauma.

Here's what's worked for me:

- David Berceli's Trauma Releasing Exercises: empowering as you can do them yourself anywhere.
- Long-term relational therapy. We heal in relationships and traditional therapy can be part of the picture.
- Bodywork: most recently Craniosacral therapy and The Rosen Method.
- Dancing 5 Rhythms regularly.
- CBD oil and good "sleep hygiene" for more restful nights.
- The work of Peter Levine and his students, like Betsy Polatin and Irene Lyon (both have other influences). I also hear good things about NARM, which is a development of Levine's work.
- Dogs.
- Paul Linden's Being-In-Movement work.

- The love of a good woman . . . and some bad ones ;-) Intimacy can heal.
- Nature generally. Forests and bodies of water especially.
- Trauma sensitive yoga for building body awareness and self-regulation.
- Martial arts done intelligently: see the work of Paul Linden.
- Trauma sensitive meditation: see David Treleaven's book.
- Helping others with trauma, but get the timing right if you're thinking of this. Don't just bring your issues to others!
- Twelve-Step Program for related addictions.
- Creative writing, others may prefer drawing, painting or other creative outlets.
- EMDR: especially good for single traumatic instances.
- Bad jokes. Really, humour helps.

The last thing I'd like to say on trauma for now is just a message of hope. If you have issues around it, while you may well not have access to all the things that have helped me, there is much you can do that really makes a difference. There are even cheap workbooks and apps that can be really useful, available online. It's work but well worth it, trust me.

There's more on trauma for facilitators in the next section.

THE BODY OF RECOVERY

– Vinnitsa, Ukraine

I'm 36. The look in the soldiers' eyes changes, as I give my talk. My fiancée Daria has asked me to come in and chat about trauma to some men she knows, who were drafted to the war in the east of Ukraine and who have come home worse for wear. I have an hour and I share what I know. Gradually, cynicism and mistrust fade, as I tell stories from Afghanistan, Sierra Leone, the Middle East, Brazil, Ethiopia and West Africa. Eyes go from empty pits, to angry, to sad, to hopeful. I pepper in lessons about trauma and PTSD that may be helpful. Afterwards, a female psychologist army officer called "Momma Tornado" hugs me goodbye and all the men shake my hand firmly. One tells me in broken English how he didn't know why he couldn't make love to his wife, or why he hits his kids since he came back home. He is determined to get help now. It's clear he's on a good path.

I met Daria while teaching therapists working in the war here. It was a bit of a set-up, actually. The war crashed the Ukrainian economy and my psychologist host wanted me to keep coming here, despite having very little money to pay me, so she had invited several attractive single women to be my interpreters in the hope I'd get involved with one of them and come back for free. Daria was used to interpreting for her dad's importing business and had also studied a lot of dance therapy. So, she took the job, none the wiser either, despite thinking it was a little strange. We were locked in a train together with nothing to do but to get to know each other for 12 hours on the way there . . . and bodies take their course. She reminds me of some weird mysterious cat-like creature.

After the talk for the soldiers, Daria and I married two days later, in her hometown, in a glitzy kitsch hotel. I woke up that morning to the sound of a small gunfight outside between some local gangsters and police. Daria and I were denied a visa for a UK wedding, but my father made it to our hastily-arranged Ukrainian alternative, and despite being very unwell, he partied hard with my Scottish uncle and the locals. Again, no shared language but love. Clare, the best friend of my first love Sally, was there too, and was clearly happy to see me happy. There were some weird Ukrainian rituals like me having to "abduct" Daria from her house, and to go under Daria's dress and get her garter belt with my teeth, at the party. Fun and games. After a honeymoon in Georgia together, where I slipped in a bathhouse and split my head open, I flew back to the UK. Daria couldn't join me which was horrible. There's power in ritual and to go against it is a crime. I was reminded of the couple from North and South Cyprus at the time. On the way home, my plane narrowly avoided crashing as there was another plane on the landing runway.

EMBODIED PEACEBUILDING

These are the notes I used for a job working with ex-combatants in Belfast. Many of those present had been in The Maze prison before the Good Friday agreement or were community leaders in Belfast. This job was a career highlight, as I'm from an Irish family with a history of people on both "sides". The job was shortly after my father's death and took place at a venue that used to be a British military barracks and housed my uncle as a soldier in the 80s.

Much is directly from my main mentor Paul Linden, who pretty much invented the field of embodied peacebuilding. This work is sorely needed and still horrifically obscure, so please spread the word.

> *"Conflict is generally experienced as threatening in some degree, and the body's reflex distress response to threats or challenges is contraction or collapse of breathing, posture, attention and move-ment – fight-flight-freeze-fold (FFFF). In situations of conflict, these powerful physical response patterns undermine people's ability to think rationally, interact empathically and act peacefully. They narrow people's choices to oppositional ways of behaving. Through balancing and opening breathing, muscle use, posture, attention and movement, people can create a state of expansiveness, calm alertness and compassionate power. These body skills enable people to stay peaceful during conflicts, which provides a foundation for resolving conflicts in harmonious and productive ways."*
>
> *– Paul Linden (taken from his book*
> Embodied Peacemaking *book)*

The scope of the body

As the body is involved in how we think, what we feel, how we perceive and how we relate, it is vital to peacebuilding. Embodied intelligence and peacebuilding can be divided into four related skill sets. Embodied peacebuilding can be done just "on" oneself or with a cooperative partner/group.

Body awareness

This is the foundation of embodied peacebuilding and requires practice, as we live in a world where trauma and technology-induced dissociation is common. Awareness is needed of both short-term state (e.g. emotions) and long-term disposition (trait).

Self-management

Centring is a way to moderate the fight-flight-freeze-fold (FFFF[33]) response, as this response makes constructive dialogue near impossible. There are many techniques, some focusing more on relaxation, expansiveness, posture or movement . . . All require awareness. The ABCC technique is one example:

- Aware: be mindful of the present moment, using the five senses and especially feel the body, notice contact with the ground (through a chair and/or the feet) and your breath.
- Balance: in posture and attention. Aim for an expansive quality.
- Core Relaxed: relax your eyes, mouth, throat, stomach and lower abdominals. Breathe deeply into your belly.
- Connect: look at or imagine others who care about you.

Embodied social awareness

We listen with our whole bodies. Various exercises can promote this. A felt empathic response to others is necessary for constructive dialogue and peacebuilding.

---

33 Note: "fold" in FFFF is also sometimes called flop, and other variations of "F's" exit in some systems, such as "friend" and "fawn".

Embodied Leadership

The foundations for this are self-awareness, self-regulation and empathy. Influence happens through the emotions and the body, as much as words. Communication is mostly non-verbal.

Psychoeducation

Stress is what happens when we perceive that the demands we face outweigh our ability to cope. It is experienced bodily. Trauma is what happens when we are exposed to something that we find deeply threatening or when we witness something horrific; it can be seen as FFFF getting "stuck". Both stress and trauma are "bio-psycho-social" and many of the reactions overlap. Resilience is our ability to "bounce back", manage stress and avoid trauma.

Trauma symptoms

These include avoidance (physical, psychological or with chemicals), hyper-arousal (e.g. anger, anxiety, sleep disturbance) and reliving (e.g. flashbacks, intrusive thoughts, nightmares). Trauma can also be linked to depression, loss of meaning, repetition compulsion (seeking danger), memory and learning problems, shame, guilt, psychosomatic illness, sexual dysfunction and relationship problems related to trust, intimacy and control. These are all embodied.

Uses for embodiment as a peacebuilder

1. Developing your own embodiment through:

    -   Long-term awareness practices
    -   Healing your own trauma and working with your own "shadow"
    -   Short-term state management, which will impact others around you

2. Methods to use with clients/participants:

- Body awareness raising (e.g. of emotions and disposition)
- Techniques for self-regulation (e.g. centring)
- Embodied coordination exercises (explicit or implicit – like singing, group movement, breath syncing, etc.)
- Embodied listening exercises
- Embodied shadow-work (e.g. moving like "them")
- Embodied yoga postures (e.g. letting go, yes and no, making a stand . . .)
- Setting up embodied "simulators" for insight (e.g. leader-follower exercises. Some examples are available on my YouTube channel (search "Mark Walsh leader follower")
- Trauma releasing exercises (EMDR, EFT, TRE . . .)

A final note

Be aware of the fundamental error: the separation of power and love as opposites. This is the mistake of thinking that love is weak, or that true power can be hateful.

EMBODIMENT AND LEADERSHIP

One of the main areas that I've worked in is developing leaders across many diverse businesses, as well as in the public and third sectors, on five continents. This has involved brief courses or work over a more extended period. Here are a few thoughts on this large topic.

A practical "how" of leadership

The first thing to say is that embodiment training *is* leadership training, as embodied capacities are the critical "soft skills" of leaders. Assuming technical expertise and intelligence (really a given in most competitive environments), it's bodymind competencies such as self-awareness, self-regulation, empathy and the ability to inspire that make the difference.

I've found that people have often read all the leadership books and maybe done an expensive MBA. However, all this does is give people a sense of what a leader *should* be like, without giving people the tools to actually develop such skills in themselves. Likewise, organisations may have nice values written on a wall, but don't live up to them – or know how to. Embodiment fills these gaps nicely and provides a practical "how" of leadership.

A long-term practice perspective is often somewhat foreign to organisations where people spend most of their time "performing" under pressure and not developing skills, and because results are often expected immediately (unlike say in sports). That being said, if embodiment is presented in the right way, then it can be embraced. The rise of emotional intelligence, mindfulness and neuroscience have helped tremendously with making embodiment accessible during the time of my career.

There is a hunger in even very mainstream organisations for genuinely interactive training. People are often *really* sick of PowerPoint and traditional training that doesn't stick. As long as you give people good reasons for doing "weird" things, and are fully at ease with them yourself, embodied training is usually well received.

Centring

Centring is often a very quick and demonstrable place to start leadership training. I find that the *no guru* and *test it for yourself* approaches work best in business. The idea of developing calm in the face of Volatile, Uncertain, Complex and Ambiguous times is very attractive, as VUCA is now regarded as the norm. A centred leader is also a persuasive and charismatic one, as nobody trusts panic!

Self-awareness

Many also already recognise the importance of self-awareness as a base for good leadership. This can quickly be increased through simple embodiment exercises like seeing someone else "do" your stance or walk, and pattern-revealing, non-athletic EYP (Embodied Yoga Principles) poses. Sometimes, I use embodied versions of familiar typologies, such as DISC and Myers-Briggs[34].

People not only learn about themselves, but gain more understanding of and empathy for others' types, which is a big advantage over traditional verbal and cognitive ways of teaching such systems, as well as being way more fun!

There are also excellent embodiment exercises for developing empathy skills (a bodily capacity after all), as well as revealing patterns in leading and following. Such an embodied approach to exploring leadership is very direct and people's tendencies quickly come out.

Embodied work brings back the heart of business

Embodied work helps people access their values, access creativity and lead from a place of depth. This is much more compelling than "head on a stick" management and that becomes very obvious to people, even after just a little training. Ethically, the "heart" of business also returns along with the body. Once they get back in contact with their bodies, I have often seen executives address corporate social responsibility, diversity and environmental concerns with a new level of passion.

This is a large topic, but I hope this piece gives a starting point. I would recommend Wendy Palmer, Richard Strozzi-Heckler (who coined the term "Embodied Leadership"), Stuart Heller and Ginny Whitelaw on this subject – all of whom have been influences.

NB: I have also written many articles and blogs on embodiment and leadership – feel free to search online!

---

34 These are the kinds of "pen and paper" personality tests common in business

THE BODY OF BUSINESS

– An office in Germany.

I'm 33. I look around the room at the smart young executives. People on their way somewhere, already on some serious money and keen to learn. I like groups like this.

There are several types of expensive mineral water on the immaculate tables. This telecoms company was one of my first well-paid international corporate clients, and I've been coming every year for a while. I followed the flow from Cyprus, trained with many people I met there, volunteered with others and learnt a trade, I guess. I'm now an embodied business trainer. I've replaced the suit I wore as a joke for my dissertation with a better one. The room is not so different from that grey day, a bit posher but still as sterile. The food at lunch is perfect and soulless.

I learnt to talk the talk. Go on, ask me about KPIs, ROIs, "churn rates", "employee engagement" or any of that bullshit. Embodied training works and it's just a matter of knowing the right words to sell it. The well-meaning HR manager here is trying to humanise the place and look after people. He's a good guy – surprisingly open minded (but you do meet a lot of closet yogis in HR and mindfulness apps are spreading). He spends his weekends on a horse ranch to de-stress. I've been working ten hours a day six days a week, to establish my company, but most of these people I train would regard that as lightweight. I've been surprised by how many lovely people I've met in business in the last few years, and have had to amend my "us and them" picture. That being said, the environments I'm now in are often brutal beyond any sanity. I make a joke about my war zone experience and how it prepared me to be here. People laugh and don't.

Natasha asks me another aggressive question – kicking the tyres of trust. She's tough, Russian, here on merit and I like her. From her file I know she has an IQ over 130, speaks 5 languages, has an MBA, has read all the leadership books . . . and it's also obvious she has almost no emotional intelligence or self-awareness. I've been told to help her or she's out, as she's in so much conflict.

What education teaches and values isn't actually what business leaders need. I tell everyone here that I assume they're clever and good at the technical aspects of their job. I ask them if they think that's enough. They then tell me about another set of skills that they have seen are important in leadership, but when I ask where they practise these skills, there's silence (I saw Richard do this in Cyprus to the aikido senseis who actually could respond). Their ears prick up when I show a study that illustrates the connection between emotional skills and salary in senior managers.

Next to Natasha is Sarah. Again, smart and technically capable at her job, which involves lots of money and Excel spreadsheets as far as I can tell. She's terminally shy however and it's holding her back. She's following my explanation of fight-flight and why we need to manage it for any logical flaw. She looks up at my slides with big brown eyes, breathing a little fuller, and I think I've got passed her scepticism.

I teach them both, and the rest of the management fast-track group, some simple centring, in non-hippie language of course, and all done sitting in chairs. We use examples like appraisals, email overload and giving presentations to help them apply it. They shift into another gear and start having conversations about ethics and the environment that I haven't heard before. They connect and share emotions for the first time as a group. They have original new ideas now that the pressure is off. To them it's a miracle just not to feel panicked by the speed of their world. To me it's another day in the body/office.

CHAPTER 7

TRAPS ON THE PATH

I've found there are some recurrent mistakes that I tend to make and traps that I see students fall into. I hope this section helps you to avoid, or at least not dwell on, some of them.[27]

WHAT WON'T HELP ON YOUR PATH TO EMBODIMENT

- Judging yourself
- Trying to be perfect
- Thinking that you've got it
- Thinking that you haven't
- A famous teacher
- Any old teacher (be selective)
- Flitting between shelves at the spiritual supermarket without committing to a path
- Getting stuck on a path
- Thinking that you can do it yourself
- Thinking that you can't
- An expensive new yoga mat (or a self-consciously old one)
- Excessive strictness/too much flow
- A new name (see also "sticking spiritual feathers up your arse and saying you're a chicken")
- Unicorn leggings
- Being vegan/paleo

27 See Portia Nelson's excellent *"Hole" poem* for another useful perspective on traps on the path.

- Going to Bali/India/wherever
- Denying your own culture and idealising another
- Penetrating your inner dolphin blow-hole with a crystal dildo, while eye-gazing your tantra teacher
- Reading this list (see also, "being a postmodern wanker")

STUPID THINGS THAT SMART PEOPLE DO

- Think being cognitively smart is what counts
- Overanalyse
- Turn wisdom into a performance or a status symbol
- Read all the books but don't practise
- Confuse knowledge with wisdom
- Have good ideas, but don't take action
- Not rest
- Believe they can plan their way out of hell
- Ruin relationships by being right
- Become "experts" and stop learning
- Write books on what can only be learnt by action

FIVE EMBODIMENT MYTHS

- You can do it on your own
- We must worship The East
- Becoming embodied is always fun
- "The body never lies"
- Yoga (or any other art) has everything that you need

I WONDER IF . . .

I wonder if we're not generally a bit quick to jump into embodied practice. To fix ourselves with yoga or whatever. I wonder if first we don't need to really mourn the grey years of numbness. To fully acknowledge the small tragedy of our own alienation. Perhaps, to be fully alive, we first need to attend our own funerals?

KEEP
CALM
IS USELESS ADVICE
UNLESS YOU HAVE
A TRAINED METHOD
FOR SELF REGULATION
AND HAVE ADDRESSED
YOUR TRAUMA HISTORY

THE ARROGANCE OF EMPATHY

Today, I visited a new yoga class, as I often do when travelling. I found the teacher subtly irritating, especially the controlling tension in her voice. Afterwards, I had dinner and the waiter left a similar bad taste in my mouth, as I felt he was subtly intrusive. These assessments were triggered by very small details, neither person was abusive and neither instance was a disaster. Both situations were an opportunity to practise gratitude and equanimity, of course, but the evening highlighted a couple of things for me.

Sensitivity can become intolerance

The first is that we can become increasingly sensitive to the embodiments of others as teachers in this field. While there are obvious benefits to this, it does risk a type of intolerance. In fact, one can think of sensitivity and equanimity[28] as two skillsets it's worth growing in proportion to each other. There's a risk we can get triggered by any little thing, otherwise!

The need for self-management and responsibility

The second thought is how, for me increasingly, subtle tones of voice indicate embodiment. An example of this is when listening to podcasts. There's a way in which I like to "taste" others, by soaking up subtle body signals (some may call this energy). This can be great for empathy and understanding others generally. However, it's also useful to turn this skill off, by self-regulating and reducing awareness of the embodiment of others. When people say, "I'm very sensitive", what they mean is that they're too sensitive in proportion to their ability to self-manage. Framing it this way brings back responsibility and takes some of the ego out of being "sensitive" as a special skill that means you can dictate to others.

---

28 A state of psychological stability, undisturbed by emotional pushing and pulling. Credit to Shinzen Young for this pairing.

It's contextual

There's also a risk of arrogance and projection in thinking one can reliably and quickly make assessments about others. When teaching embodied assessment to students (based on observation and empathy), I caution them to be aware of context and their own blind spots before jumping to conclusions. You may well be seeing or feeling the situation, not the person, and there is no "clean" place to perceive from! After teaching students The Four Elements typology, for example,[29] I sometimes hear them say things like: "He's *so* fire", when it's actually the fact that they have a strong water element, or the other person is just in a fierce mood that day. It's contextual, it's relative and we're biased.

YOGA CRACK

In my youth, aikido took over my life. I sacrificed my time, money, social life and sometimes wellbeing to an unhealthy degree to study it. I hurt myself far more studying self-defence than any mugger could have done! After some years, it *was* my life. Such obsession is not limited to the martial arts. Many others also seem under the control of their art. I have seen meditators squander their inheritance on years of retreats, yogis choosing to live in poverty to maintain their regular stretch high, and conscious dancers ruin careers with endless workshops and ecstatic late nights. When you *have* to do something, it can no longer be said to be a mindfulness practice, it's a compulsion.

Practices can be truly addictive. I don't mean addictive as in "I really like and benefit from it, so I do it a lot". I mean as in literally being reliant upon an internally-generated, drug-like high that ruins everything else you care about and colonises your life. It basically makes everything else smaller and smaller, resulting in the death of all that you love. I say this as an ex-addict/alcoholic, so I don't make the comparison lightly.

---

29 Search "Mark Walsh 4 Elements" on YouTube for visual demonstrations.

Addictions are often defined by two criteria:

1. You do it compulsively when you say you won't.
2. It negatively impacts the things that you value in your life.

While bodymind practices are, of course, enriching and beneficial too – hence this book (and are the basis of many wonders in my own life), it is worth asking if an art has parasitised your life. Not sure? Why not take a month off and see? You could quit any time, right? ;-)

TO SUFFER IS NOT TO BENEFIT

There's a deeply held, implicit belief that we must suffer to grow. It's Christian essentially but has made its way into most aspects of bodymind practice and personal growth. Today, extreme hot yoga, hardcore ultra-ultra-marathons and full-on ice training are some of the most popular methods of nobly torturing oneself. Much of this practice has an almost sadomasochistic quality[30]; and numb people get addicted to extreme sensation, so they can feel again. The notion that it must be doing some good if it's uncomfortable is hard to shake! Gentler classic practices like Feldenkrais and The Alexander Technique remain somewhat obscure, even when they give demonstrable results.

This is the dark side of sacrifice. While there is often worth in giving something up (and I frequently see people benefit more from my courses when there is a greater time/energy/financial commitment), suffering doesn't always create value! To suffer is not to benefit. I'm thinking of starting Hell Yoga™, where I pointlessly torture people to make some money and prove a point.

This is not to say, of course, that challenge is a waste of time. Intensity that's carefully calibrated to people's skill can create a "sweet spot" for learning self-regulation, discipline and the forging of one's will. I have done this; it has value for the soft, liberal, coddled modern world

---

30 But please don't hear that I'm devaluing the kink scene, which in fact can be an exceptional place to learn about boundaries, consent and embodiment, if done consciously. The kink world was actually well ahead of the rest of us in many regards.

especially. However, simply suffering is not helpful. Most people I've worked with use intensity to reinforce a narrative of low self-worth and punishment, to further disembody and avoid coming home. More often, what is helpful is a gentle, forgiving listening, a returning home to the abandoned lover of the body. Fuck, it took me 20+ years of martial arts, extreme sports and kinky sex to work this out, though! It's deeply countercultural.

However, alongside the intelligently challenging, there is also a place for the occasionally unreasonable. I have a few "war stories" from extreme martial arts practices, for example. I'm glad that, as a young man, I pushed myself to some seemingly insane edges, which exist far beyond where most people think they do. I would recommend this occasionally for the testosterone-driven and the very dedicated who wish to become professionals in the field of embodiment. A few of us must descend into hell to steal fire from the Gods, but this is not sustainable or a healthy bodily norm.

This exception aside, I'd encourage you to be a rebel: to *not* push yourself. Delight in the pleasure of your body. Be fucking kind to yourself. Gentle is the new extreme!

THE MANNER AND THE METHOD

How you do any embodied practice is at least as important as *what* you do to develop yourself.

The way you do something can undermine or enhance its potential benefits. The definition of "how" is actually close to a definition of "embodiment", so this is hardly surprising.

How is often the manner in which our own habits reassert themselves and resist change. Rushing to yoga, obsessing and being controlling about free dance, even angrily doing kindness meditation are all traps I've fallen into!

Focus on the manner, as well as the method. The medium is the message!

STATE TYRANNY VERSUS STATE LEADERSHIP

We all learn to regulate ourselves (to a greater or lesser degree), by using both internal and external means. This is a good thing of course, but we can overdo this and become pseudo-calm centring robots, meditation control-freaks or fake yoga transcenders. Power over our feelings can become a type of tyranny, where we inhibit and dominate ourselves. The leash becomes too short and then often snaps, of course.

Another possibility is to *lead* our states, but only after first really listening to the message of our emotions (for example, if we're angry because someone has violated us, or scared because we're in danger, this is worth being aware of!). We can also allow ourselves to be human, give ourselves a break and just express how we are, freely – in a way that means we and others will not be harmed. This is not the same as just being a bloody baby that cries at every little thing and confuses being ill-disciplined and badly regulated with being free though. Balance is key as with most things.

THE REAL MAGIC

Special skills (real and imagined) are very attractive. The promise of learning advanced sexual alchemy, shooting Reiki energy from your fingers like a benevolent Yoda, having the ninja death touch or the psychic skills to see what mere mortals cannot – and a host of other things – is seductive.

People can make a lot of money offering such tricks, as there's a huge appetite for them. I could do this too, but choose not to.

What I notice in myself though, is that there is a desire to learn such things, but that it reeks of ego: a need to be special, to impress and control others, to be unique. It's a natural, childish urge to be noteworthy and have power over others. To use magic to be safe and grand. Who doesn't want to be Harry Potter or Luke Skywalker?

I want to make a case for inclining oneself to the skills of a normal human adult. Simply being competent is challenge enough for a lifetime. This takes a certain honesty and humility.

My real learning edge involves things like only eating when hungry and resting when I'm tired. Being nice to customer service people when frustrated. Listening to my wife. Showing up on time to work and doing the job well. This is enough.

Not so sexy. Not so good for impressing people . . . but the real deal. Ordinary competence is the real magic.

BE AWARE OF THE FLOW

"Go with the flow" usually means doing what's easy; going with habitual, addictive patterns; not honouring your word, and having no sense of commitment.

Then there's the deep flow of what you're genuinely, deeply, intuitively called to; dancing within the context of adult responsibility.

Learn to tell the difference.

BEING AUTHENTIC IS LIKE WILD SEX

If you think you're doing it, you're not. The same could be said for embodiment: you can't think that you're embodied.

EMBODIMENT IS ORDINARY

Embodiment is profoundly ordinary. If you're wearing your embodiment as a technicolour jacket to impress, dominate or feel superior to others, it is not embodiment. Embodiment is not an identity, not a fashion, and not a fucking hashtag.

THE MISUSES, ABUSES AND TRAVESTIES OF EMBODIMENT

I have made an impassioned case in this book that coming home to our bodies will make the world a better place. This is fundamentally true, and yet it is important not to be naive and to heed the lessons made obvious from what has happened to the modern secular mindfulness movement, and other parallels. The main danger actually comes from what in Buddhism are known as the "near enemies" of embodiment.

Sometimes the idea is misunderstood, or simply misused, as the word becomes fashionable and therefore profitable. Here are a few things that embodied practitioners should take care to avoid, and that as a community we should be vigilant of.

Embodiment isn't any damn thing

Embodiment is many things, but it isn't anything [waves to goat/beer yoga]. People may place the line differently, but it's important to have one. In my view, if a practice isn't body awareness based and focused on developing the person who is practising, it isn't an embodied art. Knowing what is and isn't an embodied practice matters, hence I am including a whole chapter on this subject. Frankly, I fear that the word will be used for any old BS and I see signs of this already in some circles as people cash in, or just want to sound cool as "embodiment' trends as a word.

Travesties vs. gateway drugs

Arts that look like they are always embodied, such as yoga, can not only not be this (e.g. if 'merely bad gymnastics'), but can actually be travesties. While I don't mind activities that are not so deep but ultimately lead people into more embodied arts (acting as "gateway drugs," I like to joke), I do mind those which lead people away from them. Embodiment travesties are activities which actively numb people while claiming to be embodied. Such abominations may involve such strenuous activity, such neurotic forms, such authoritarian teaching, or such faux-spiritual body denialism that they actively disconnect people from their bodies. It is hard to feel, when all your attention is on surviving, or on getting it right for the teacher or an imagined spiritual ideal, rather than reality. See my e-book Making Yoga Meaningful for more on this.

Crutches, compensations, escapism and enabling

I have seen people become reliant on embodied practices to the point where they use them as crutches for underdeveloped skills, e.g. getting great at centring to deal with bad social skills rather than gaining better social skills. Embodiment can also become enabling whereby people use it to abuse themselves more, say using yoga to push past what is a sensible and kind workload; or even to feel better about abusing others by blissing out on practices. You feel bad about working in a meaning-less soul-crushing that job you hate? Don't worry, take this meditation pill and go on this dance holiday! State highs make great escapism and one can drug oneself in order to cope, rather than use practices to con-nect and learn. People can also learn to perform embodied arts really well as a compensation for being terrible at life, taking solace in their perfect hip-throw or triangle pose, while their job and marriage are disasters, and they're achieving nothing. Brutal to say it, but I see it.

More efficient arseholes

There were senior Nazis who did yoga, and the atrocious Imperial Japanese Army of World War Two widely practiced and was supported by Japanese Zen. More recently, modern mindfulness taught indepen-dently of any ethics has been taken up by everyone from corporations with no social values, to snipers, to pickup artists; to improve their main activities. It is possible to use embodied practices to make ourselves more efficient at whatever we do, including bad things . . . though it is often the near enemy of transcending the body (and therefore empa-thy), or those missing relational practices, that are the prime culprits for simply sharpening the knife of evil. True embodied practise is safer ethically as it turns on our capacity to feel the pain of others, so we are less likely to infect it.

I hope that this book goes some way to deterring some of the pos-sible misuses of embodiment and pseudo "embodiment", but people are people, and time will tell!

CHAPTER 8

FOR THE PROFESSIONALS

This section is for anyone who works as, or wishes to be, an embodied facilitator of any kind. This could mean being a yoga, dance or martial arts teacher, a coach, bodyworker or even just a leader in the widest possible sense, as many sections will apply to anyone who works with people. We've gotten really geeky about this stuff on the Embodied Facilitator Course (EFC) and learnt much of this over the years in the UK and Russia as a team; so thank you to all the EFC trainers for gathering this wisdom, especially Francis Briers, Rachel Blackman and Alexandra Vilvovskaya.

HOW TO HELP SOMEONE WHO'S SUFFERING

This is from a resilience workshop I led for managers. It's super simple, but possibly profound. Usually people try a limited range of these approaches or have a strong habit to. They're also in a progressive order, so you can think of this as an options "ladder".

- Get your own shit together, both for role modelling and the capacity to help. Centre yourself first.
- Check your motivation before getting involved.
- Listen, if they want to talk.
- Offer empathy, not sympathy. This usually comes before more seemingly active steps.
- Reframe the situation to encourage responsibility and acceptance, if they're open to that. This could mean steering away from apathy or self-hatred. NB: it could be aggravating for someone, if what they want is solely empathy.

- Touch them, if they want touch (and if it's not about easing your discomfort with their suffering). It can be soothing or invigorating, to suit the individual and situation.
- Coach them or try creative problem solving, if they want help but don't know what they need. This is usually better than advice; offer that *only* if directly asked and you are qualified.
- Encourage or challenge them, to fit the individual and situation; again, with permission.
- Offer direct, practical help, if they need it (fix their car, kill their enemies, etc). Only offer this when they can't do something themselves or can't learn to. Teach them, if you can, whilst helping.

TOP TIPS FOR FACILITATORS

I have been working with other embodied facilitators for some years, this is most of what I know condensed into a short list!

- Know what you're trying to do. Clear aims matter.
- Being is more important than tools. Embody what you're teaching.
- Any training is a cycle. The beginning is not the middle, and the middle is not the end. This flow matters, for example building trust and authority early, and helping people get clear take-aways and "come down" ready for outside life, at the end.
- Give clear instructions, involving a "how" that a ten-year-old could grasp.
- Speak the truth. I don't just mean, "don't lie".
- Have a plan.
- Listen and adapt what you're doing in the present moment. Don't just follow a plan or do yesterday's training.
- Take what you do seriously, but don't take yourself seriously. Humour is a powerful tool.
- Don't fuck anyone that you're teaching or take advantage of them financially.
- Culture matters. We're not all the same and American showmanship or a sensitive Californian style won't work most places.
- A little love goes a long way.

SEVEN WAYS THE BODY GIVES COACHING SUPERPOWERS

Many coaches have a vague sense that the body is important in their work, but may not be aware of exactly how much it matters or, practically, how to work with it. I've spent many years helping other coaches increase their embodied skills, and for the last few years this has been my main focus[35].

Here's a quick list of some of the most important reasons not to ignore the body.

1. **It tells you what you're broadcasting**
    Your bodily states and general disposition are always transmitting to others. Your body is "screaming" and our bodily ways of being are one of the most dramatic influences on clients, regardless of the words we are speaking. Learning about this is vital.

2. **It's your super-Google**
    While logical techniques and tools are helpful, it's only by accessing deep bodily wisdom and intuition that we can do our best work.

3. **It's your free legal high**
    Simple bodily techniques, such as centring, can be used to quickly self-regulate and relax (or wake up), when faced with the challenges of coaching and facilitation.

4. **It's your X-ray specs**
    Your own body is shouting a story of your history and dispositions, and so do your clients' bodies. By becoming more embodied yourself, you can more accurately assess and adapt to clients, both in marketing and delivery.

5. **It makes you and your clients Transformers**
    If you develop a greater embodied range for yourself and then teach clients to do the same, new possibilities quickly open. By

35 See also the EFC website for more tips, videos and free resources for coaches. https://embodiedfacilitator.com/

being able to step into new ways of being, we quickly see new ways to do things and new solutions to problems.

6. **It's your psychic spy**
    By tuning into your own body when coaching, you will become aware of how it mirrors others, giving you vital information about a client or group, for example when they are feeling uncomfortable. In this way, you can intuit far more, which of course makes you better able to facilitate.

7. **It makes you human!**
    Being tuned into yourself makes you authentic, ethical and in touch with what you care about. If we aren't bringing that fully into our work, what's the point? Being embodied is being human.

THE NECESSARY FOUNDATION

Ten thousand+ hours of embodied teaching across fifty countries has taught me something of the key conditions for transformational embodied work. There's a universal set of conditions that help people "open up", "dive in" or whatever cheesy metaphor you like for getting real and doing the work. These really apply to any relationship-building activity, but are particularly vital if you want intimacy or the necessary conditions for significant personal growth. Sometimes people talk about "safety", which I don't like. It's too vague and tends towards a kind of soft, new age, politically correct tyranny that I can't stand and don't think is helpful. But maybe that's just a personal terminological preference and much of what I outline below is especially helpful for those with trauma. In any event, here are some concrete foundations that will be useful to build, if you have any interest in working with people at all. I teach them to Embodied Facilitator Course (EFC) and Embodied Yoga Principles (EYP) teachers, as pass-fail criteria for teacher trainings as a I regard them as so important.

Six universal conditions

1. Choice
Don't keep slaves. Consent matters. Give options. Choice teaches agency and shows respect.

2. Commonality
People must see what they have in common with you and others in the group. There should be a sense of belonging, including shared experiences and values. Often you can just point this out. At twelve-step groups like AA, they say, "Look for the similarities, not the differences". My favourite is to ask, "Anyone here not gonna die one day?" Another good one is, "Who doesn't have any stress in their lives?"

3. Predictability
Tell people what's happening and what's going to happen. This makes the future less threatening. Be reliable. Be fair. Back up agreed rules.

4. Authority and equality
You need to both establish subject matter authority and create a sense of personal equality. The ideal balance between the two is pretty culturally determined, and is shown in many small ways. You can show authority by being well-introduced or mentioning your past clients, for example; and equality by waiting in line for lunch or also wearing a name badge, even though everyone knows who you are. These things may seem trivial but such implicit messages matter.

5. Serve
With every action ask, "Is this for me or for them?"

6. A sense of humour
Take note overly sincere new agers and fundamentalists left and right: humour creates space to grow, and distance from unhealthy patterns.

These foundations are all embodied of course. For instance, being relaxed shows expertise far more than verbal humble bragging.

THE TEN PRINCIPLES OF EMBODIED EDUCATION

These ten principles form a pithy reminder of much of what's in this book. In fact as stated here, these principles are so condensed that they could appear as riddles. While seemingly simple, they take years to understand deeply and to apply skilfully.

1. Bi-directionality holography
The body both creates and reveals our way of being, and one aspect shows all others (holography).

2. Context
Our current situation, relationships, culture, disposition and the environment are all embodied. We are layered adaptations to context and history.

3. Comfort
Familiarity reveals what's habitual. We feel "at home" in what we have practised, and it feels easy.

4. Joy
Delight reveals what's needed or longed for, including what brings meaning and our values.

5. Deviation
Inability to follow a form (for example a set of dance moves or a yoga pose) reveals habitual patterns. Habits assert themselves unconsciously and are exposed by form.

6. Guidance
The body can guide our life. When listened to, the body gives wisdom. Not to be confused with comfort!

7. Practice
We are always practising, unconsciously or consciously, and become what we practise. We can learn to embody new ways of being over time through an intelligently designed programme.

8. Contrast
The body reveals and learns by exaggeration, contrast and embodied differentiation. By enhancing the differences between two things, those things become clearer.

9. Relationship
We learn in relationship. By being witnessed and naming something to others we deepen insight and declare new futures.

10. Integration
We can transfer embodied learning into daily life, by identifying micro-indicators of pattern, and micro-movements/poses, or by shifting these.

Supplemental principles

11. Process
The body is a process (verb) and it benefits us to listen and follow.

12. Self-regulation
The fight-flight-freeze (FFF) and craving[36] responses can be managed through relaxation, expansiveness and structural alignment.

13. Trigger
Shadow is revealed by triggering and infatuation.

14. Chaos
The body is free and has no laws!

Developed for Embodied Yoga Principles and through teaching The Embodied Facilitator Course, drawing from Paul Linden, Richard Strozzi-Heckler, Wendy Palmer, Stuart Heller, Ginny Whitelaw and Dylan Newcomb. The vast majority of embodied training works explicitly or implicitly with these principles.

---

36 Much embodied work follows the Western tradition of working with an aversive (FFF) response, but fails to recognise the grasping/craving response, which is very similar, but triggered by what we like! Surprisingly, these two responses are very similar physiologically. Buddhism of course works with both aversion and craving.

VERBAL MISTAKES TO AVOID WHEN TEACHING EMBODIMENT

These are the most common verbal mistakes I see people in this field make:

- Giving possible outcomes and metaphors, rather than clear methods, e.g. "Empty your mind", or, "Have a mind like water", versus "Bring your attention to the physical sensations of breathing". This is known as non-operational language, as the clear method is missing and it forces people to guess what you'd actually like them to do!
- Starting instructions with, "Just . . ." This is a common verbal tic, which minimises the task, which may not be easy or trivial to your participants.
- Use of foreign, "spiritual" or anatomical/scientific jargon, as a way of claiming status; it often only makes things less unclear.
- Using an annoying breathy spiritual "yoga/dance voice" or even a different accent! Just speak normally! More broadly, practice use of tone matters, as this conveys your own embodiment.
- Use of "good", "nice" and other value judgements, which suggest certain options are better than others (assuming you don't want to do this). For example, "nice and deep into the stretch", implying that it's somehow better to go deep than not. Value judgements may be inherent in word choices such as, "Collapse the chest", which sounds bad compared to, "Flex the upper spine"!
- Asking questions such as, "What happened in your body?" This frames people as passive victims of their own bodies. A better question that encourages personal responsibility would be, "What did you do in your body?".
- Telling participants what they are seeing/experiencing and not letting them spot it for themselves, for example, "You are feeling relaxed". Letting people spot it for themselves teaches them self-observation and responsibility for their own bodies.
- Not giving a reason for an exercise. This encourages blind faith, as opposed to healthy questioning.
- Forgetting to ask permission when touching. Or alternatively, asking but not really being okay with a "no". This creates compliance.

The ethical way is to gain explicit verbal consent, or at least a non-verbal indicator.[37]

- Use of demands. Obviously, this is disempowering. I do not believe it is always necessary to make it explicit that a request not a demand is being made – e.g. by saying, "please" (!), "I invite you", "if you like" or by giving options, but it is a good idea to do this sometimes especially early on with a group. Tone conveys a lot but what is most critical in the request-demand distinction is how you treat anyone who doesn't agree to your request!

- Use of "we" when no agreement is made. This is an example of "forced teaming", as opposed to gaining consent. For example: "We are doing X now" (also a fait accompli).

- "Next you'll . . ." This is another example of a fait accompli. Again, it removes the chance for participants to give consent. Instead, you could offer alternatives, support people who choose to not follow your lead and actively teach students to say "no".

Some of these may seem like nit-picking and I'm pretty obsessed with the stuff to be fair, but these are more important than they may seem. That being said, it's your embodiment that matters most and I've seen great teachers give *terrible* instructions, but with huge love, and their trainings still be ethical and effective. Others say the nicest things but filled with venom! Intent, tone and how things are received trump the exact words, and there are times when I would break many of these rules, so it's situational too (for example in some cultural contexts, where too much choice may actually make people feel anxious).

---

37 Trickily neither verbal nor non-verbal indicators of consent can be fully trusted as many people have been conditioned to try and please irrespective of their actual wishes. I teach students to err on the side of caution however and take a maybe (e.g. when someone says yes but flinches) as a no. The key thing is really that facilitators are consent aware and tuned into an ethic of consent, not that a rigid rule is applied.

COACHING, TRAINING AND TRAUMA

This section on trauma is useful reading for any trainer or coach, as it describes some of the signs and symptoms of trauma and the effects it can have on learning. It's ideal for people new to the area and may be too simple for those already experts.

Perhaps the first thing to say is that trauma is incredibly common. For example, statistics show an 80% lifetime prevalence of traumatic incidence in the UK and in the USA; and some claim one-in-four women and one-in-six men has been sexually assaulted or abused. Trauma symptoms, if not recognised, are potentially undermining to any learning situation, so are well worth knowing about. Being a trauma-aware facilitator also correlates very highly with just being an effective one; creating a sense of safety is an excellent educational foundation for all, especially when it comes to deeper or transformational learning.

A little personal background

As well as being a business trainer and coach, I am a trauma educator. I've trained therapists, humanitarian workers and businesspeople in trauma and psychological resilience. I have worked in many places: with the military in Sierra Leone, The House of Lords of the Parliament of the United Kingdom, The Metropolitan Police in London and in war zones. I have also been through a personal trauma journey from PTSD (Post Traumatic Stress Disorder) to recovery.

"Trauma" is a word that's now thrown around very easily, so I want to be clear that I refer to it in its clinical sense, i.e. an experience of overwhelm involving threat to life or the integrity of self. Sadly, abuse, rapes, car accidents, assaults . . . are part of many people's life experience and while many recover from the acute (short term) psychological symptoms, a proportion develop longer term symptoms. These are sometimes grouped as disorders, such as generalised anxiety disorder and PTSD.

Below, I've listed some of the more common groupings of symptoms that can be trauma-related generally, and I've described how they relate to facilitation.

Possible trauma-related symptoms in a coaching context

Hyperarousal
Being stuck in fight-flight-freeze (FFF) mode is a core trauma symptom, which expresses in different ways, including anxiety (the loss of a sense of safety is key to much trauma), anger and irritability, concentration issues, difficulty listening, hyper-vigilance (being always on the lookout), emotional sensitivity and sleeplessness. For a trainee/client with such issues, sitting still to learn may be difficult, as may traditional mindfulness or being asked to access emotions (though these can be healing, if done right). Such a person may seem overly fearful to participate due to perceived emotional threat. A lack of ability in regulating emotions is a common trauma symptom and this can easily show up in any learning process, especially when there is insufficient trust, for example when HR have forced them to be in a training, or a manager is there. Traumatised participants could also seem "difficult", aggressive or confrontational.

Physical and emotional numbing
Trauma can make people numb, as this is a way to cope with overwhelming physical or emotional pain. This can lead to all sorts of health issues as well as emotional issues, which can show up in training. A lack of empathy or insensitivity to others' emotions may be trauma related. Critically, trauma often damages attachment, boundaries, trust and relationships generally. Trauma is toxic to intimacy and relationships, including learning relationships (such as the coaching one). Think of trainees who can't say no, always want to please you, don't trust the trainer, want to get too close immediately, can't let go of a group after a session ends or who don't respect other boundaries. Such issues may be trauma related.

Avoidance
If a person has been traumatised by something, they likely want to avoid it. This can apply to situations they read as similar. Examples of this include linking bomb explosions to any loud bangs, or linking a rapist to all people of the same ethnicity. In a training, if someone has a very strong, unexplained reaction against doing something, this may be avoidance and it's best to respect it. Paradoxically, people can also develop "repetition compulsion", where in an unconscious attempt to

heal, they re-expose themselves to something similar to what trauma-tised them. If you do "extreme" and intense personal development, you may well encounter such people.

Intrusive symptoms

Intrusive symptoms include someone constantly thinking about a trau-matic event against their will, which can be very distracting to learning. Or less commonly, the famous dissociative "flashbacks", when a person is unaware of the present and thinks they are back in the traumatic situation. Traumatic memories are different from regular ones and are very "alive" in a person, even when deliberately remembered. Intrusive symptoms can be triggered by seemingly harmless stimuli, for example the smell of a cigarette reminding a survivor of a house fire.

What a trainer or coach can do

In trauma, what's damaged is the ability to easily meet core emotional/ relational needs. Building trust, belonging and safety are part of any good facilitator's skills and this is the key to working with people with trauma backgrounds. This may be something as simple as introducing a new delegate who arrives late, or asking how people are and what they need to be able to learn in their own way.

Some other specifics might include:

- Being aware of, on the lookout for, and compassionate towards trauma symptoms.
- Know competent therapists and refer when in doubt. People with trauma often come to coaching, as it is less stigmatised than ther-apy, but if someone presents to you with serious untreated trauma and you are not a trauma therapist, refer them to a specialist. Know the limits of your expertise.
- Trainings that are active (but also teach some self-regulatory tech-nique like centring) can be easier for people with hyper-arousal symptoms.
- Be impeccable with touch, boundaries, ethics and consent. I see a lot of trainers doing techniques or touching people without explicit permission. Don't! And if in doubt, a maybe is a no. Traumatised

people may have bad boundaries, so it is your responsibility to behave ethically.

- Many coaches and trainers get into the work after difficult circumstances. However, it is essential that a facilitator works on their own trauma, if they have it, so as not to damage others by acting out unhealthy patterns. Being in ongoing therapy/super-vision is advisable.
- Be careful of potential triggers and respect people's avoidance patterns.
- Know that long-term trauma can heal and can even lead to growth (most acute trauma symptoms heal on their own actually).

Effective treatment methods

While you shouldn't attempt to apply them if you're untrained, it is good to know that effective trauma treatments exist. Personally, I see trauma as physical, social, psychological and spiritual, so the best healing includes all these elements. Effective treatments are listed below:

- Cognitive Behavioural Therapy (UK NICE[38] guideline approved)
- EMDR – an eye movement technique (UK NICE guideline approved)
- Trauma Releasing Exercises
- Emotional Freedom Technique (controversial, but I know experts who swear by it)
- Somatic Experiencing, Hakomi, NARM and other bodily approaches
- Self-help books (such as *8 Keys to Safe Trauma Recovery* by Babette Rothschild)

Conclusion

Trauma exists, it's common and it's affecting your training/coaching already. I hope this little bit of information has helped. There's a world more out there, as it's a growing field.

---

38 The National Institute for Health and Care Excellence – a UK governmental organisation that assess treatments for public funding.

HOW NOT TO SEEM LIKE A BLOODY HIPPIE WHEN WORKING WITH NORMAL PEOPLE

I've been successfully bringing unusual embodied practices into what could be called "mainstream" environments for over 15 years now, working with everyone from large corporate entities (such as Unilever, Shell and L'Oréal), to the police and international military units. I've also worked with other potentially "hard" audiences, such as humanitarian aid workers in war zones and sceptical young people from inner cities. While these groups are diverse, what they have in common is that they don't suffer fools gladly, and that they enjoy a pragmatic approach. I sometimes joke that my job is, "Doing weird stuff with normal people", however, I hold the "normal versus hippie" thing very lightly, as obviously it's a bit of a joke. These days weirdly, in many ways, I relate better to the mainstream groups I teach than to the "alternative" world that spawned me.

So, here are my top tips for bringing crazy, "hippie" stuff to people that will really benefit from it, in a way that they can stomach.

See what you have in common

While it's easy to go into 'us and them' mode with any group (and this piece plays with that), I try to notice what I have in common with 'them'. Yes, they may be executives or whatever, but we're all human. Even really unlikely people share at least some of your values and life experiences, if you see past the packaging.

Speak to concerns and have a clear aim

To sell any kind of alternative course, such as meditation or yoga, you'll need to speak to the client's concerns. What's in it for them? They likely don't care that it's your favourite hobby. They want real results for their real lives. What is the benefit of what you do? Similarly, when doing a course, it's vital to have a clear aim for any session and any exercise.

People will try all kinds of weird shit if they have a good reason that links to their values.

Get operational

When you give instructions for an exercise, state the method, not a metaphor or a potential result. Tell people the "how". For example, say, "Bring your attention to the physical sensations of breathing", as opposed to, "Empty your mind". Do not tell people to, "Extend their energy to the corners of the universe", or whatever, even if this makes sense to you. If in doubt, check your instructions with a ten-year-old, who isn't afraid to say when you make no sense.

Kill your unicorns

Most alternative subcultures have developed their own jargon and ways of speaking, which are actually repulsive to many normal people. My students hunt and kill words and phrases such as "energy", "drop into" and "holding space". We playfully call these "unicorns". If in doubt, ask, "Would this word or phrase appear in a conservative newspaper?" or "Would my boring uncle use it?" Alternatively, you can employ the helpful kid from before, and pay them for every unicorn they catch you using!

Stop floating and flowing

It's not just what you do and say, but how you do it and say it that matters.[39] A facilitator's embodiment can undermine their message. To use the four elements model introduced earlier in the book, generally I see "alternative" people embodying too much water and air, and not enough earth and fire (i.e. not being firm, organised or direct enough). This can prevent them connecting with mainstream groups who tend to be

---

39 This could be a good definition of an embodied approach to leadership in fact!

earth and fire heavy (though of course not always, a group of HR mangers for example may be more watery).

Look at your relationship to money and power

Having issues around these two themes undermine people from alternative subcultures time and time again, either because of beliefs (e.g. "Rich people aren't good people") or more subtly, (e.g. somehow never having any money despite earning plenty). These themes can be explored and cleaned up. More broadly, therapeutic "shadow work" is essential for any facilitator. Working with mentee EFC graduates I have found it can take some time to "clean up" these issues, even among very developed people.

Be reliable (for God's sake!)

Keep your word. Do what you say. Be on time and be impeccable with your promises. This is a big deal in many mainstream subcultures and reliability will go a long way. No. Excuses.

Dress the part

It's a simple one, but when in Rome, chuck on a toga. You can still be you (in fact, being 10% weirder than your clients is a plus, that's what they got you in for quite often), but don't wear tie-dye or a sarong. I normally just ask a client, "What do people normally wear to trainings here?" and adjust accordingly. Dressing the part will help you blend in enough to open people's ears.

Remember what you bring to the party

With all this trying to blend in, sometimes people forget that they've been brought into such places precisely because they're different or have different skills. Yes, adapt and accommodate, but not when it comes to key values. Own the awesome you have that they need.

Conclusion

I hope this introduction saves you some time and tears, so you don't need to work it out the hard way, like I did. The world really needs to get its heart, body and soul back, and some of the alternative arts can help – and let's not get in the way of that message. This works both ways, as much can be learnt from mainstream cultures too (my own journey in running a business for example has been profound).[40]

HEALTH CHECK-UP FOR EMBODIMENT TEACHERS

Here are some challenging questions to teachers in embodied fields. Ask them to yourself if teaching, or use them as a checklist for current and new teachers. Given the huge number of guru scandals and abuse cases in recent years in some embodiment fields (e.g. within yoga), a list like this is long overdue:

- Are you controlling or empowering students? Are they dependent on you?
- How do you know your students can say no to you? If you do not know this, how do you know that you're not abusing them? When was the last time they challenged you on something and you admitted you were wrong?
- What systemic checks and balances are in place to manage your ego and personality flaws? Can you list your top three personality flaws and how they may lead to trouble? Do you have a therapist to work on those?
- Are you subject to the same rules as those in your organisation? A.k.a. The Magna Carta principle.
- Is there a clear ethical framework for your work? Who keeps you accountable for it? Do you have a mentor and supervisor?
- Are you responsible in how you change the state of your students? Do you addict them to highs or create real life insight and skills?

---

40 This piece is a condensed version of a free e-book available on the EFC site https://embodiedfacilitator.com/shop.

- Is anything you say true just because you say it?
- Are you empire-building and is this what the world needs more of?
- If democracy is something you value, how do you democratise this work? Can you be outvoted to make sure you don't make abusive or just stupid decisions?
- Will your students one day be better than you and are you happy about it if so?
- How do you make the work accessible to more than a few? Are you creating social change or just making elites more efficient and comfortable in their position?
- Are you clear on the scope of your work and what is not your work? Do you regularly say, "I'm not qualified to give advice on that."?
- Are you trained in consent culture? It's important and not as obvious as it may seem. Things have changed a lot in the last few years in this area.
- Do you have awareness of, and education in, diversity and inclusion issues? Note: this does not mean fully taking on the current West Coast/far-left/postmodern view and language, but to have considered these issues and spent time developing one's understanding for different group's challenges and needs.
- Can we really teach embodiment well from a sense of lack and scarcity? Are you copyrighting and trademarking to fence off a small corner of this field? Are we really so poor as to just protect our little piece of the pie?

On the last point: we have to make a living of course and I appreciate it isn't always easy. However, there are now ways to have your cake and share it too. By giving, we get. Modern marketing and spiritual wisdom are surprisingly aligned. The internet can scale our skills and offer much to people for free. Peer-to-peer is the future. Empowering students and putting this work out there benefits us all.

I have just "open sourced" the Embodied Yoga Principles system meaning that anyone can use it, which I see as both a stand for a desirable way of living, and also just common sense and good business, in a age where nothing can be controlled anyway, and where profit comes from letting good ideas spread.

THERE IS NO AUTHORITY IN EMBODIMENT

There is no authority in embodiment.

The embodied fields access truth through direct experience only. That's it.

What such and such important teacher said is at best a guide (yeah, me included). Lineages and traditions are pointers, but frankly a lot of them are full of crap. Giving authority to a guru is disempowering, dangerous and misses the core method of any embodied field. Status doesn't matter.

A practice being old ("ancient teaching" my arse) or brand new, isn't relevant.

How many years you've made the same mistake over and over again isn't relevant.

Whether a practice comes from another supposedly more "spiritual" culture isn't relevant. Stop with the fucking Sanskrit, Japanese, Tibetan, etc. You're just adding a layer of complication. Again, it's just status claiming.

Put your bloody brain scan images away too. Neuroscience doesn't prove shit; it just describes it another way (that isn't helpful for embodied practice). Focusing on what "science says" reeks of insecurity (and it's very likely you're not qualified, anyway).

Now, I don't want to suggest a kind of obnoxious, teenage postmodernism in all this. It's not "just my opinion", and there are differing experience levels. I am, however, making a case for experiential learning, being the centre of embodied arts.

CHAPTER 9

FURTHER CONSIDERATIONS

The following are a few extras that could be considered "advanced" considerations for those already deeply into this work. Skip it if newer to embodiment, or come back to it in a few years if you like.

EMBODIED CONTEXTS

Here's something that's usually not considered when connecting with people across the globe virtually: the differing embodied contexts we're physically in create a disconnect. I had this insight talking to a friend in Goa yesterday. I felt the difference between tropical India and rainy Brighton as a subtle barrier between us.

While reading this, you're in a different place and a different time to me. This means that there are different forces working on you now than on me. Your context is different, so you're different. We don't have a shared embodied substrate to help smooth the differences between us. It's really quite strange and humans didn't evolve for it.

DON'T LISTEN TO YOUR BODY – Aka the body always lies

As an embodiment teacher, I've been encouraging people to get in touch with their bodily selves, and therefore their values, compassion and intuition, for years. Recently however, I've started to hear people say that their reason for doing some piece of bullshit or another, was because they, "listened to their bodies".

While the body can be a source of deep wisdom, its primary response to any situation is conditioned craving and aversion: basically being a jerk. Greed, fear and anger tend to be what we tune into in the first instance and being pushed around by these forces isn't so great. Without the ability to self-regulate and listen deeper than the fight-flight-freeze (FFF) response, well . . . you're just being bossed around by your inner toddler. Well done, hippie.

It's also just a great excuse. When I asked a social justice princess why she engaged in some obnoxious behaviour recently, or when someone else I know broke a promise and I challenged them on it, their responses that they, "listened to their bodies", was a great fucking get-out clause. You can't really reason with that, right? There's no discussion because there's no logic or further evidence needed. It's like a new, "God says I'm right".

So, listen to your body, yes – but with great care. It's easy to fool yourself or to use the body as a scapegoat for shitty decisions, if not.

THE NEW BARONS OF TRAUMA

When I started learning about trauma, it was an unusual thing to be aware of in embodied communities. I'd come across the realities of it when doing humanitarian work in various war zones, so had become interested in it personally. My main mentor, Paul Linden, happened to specialise in this field too. His work with aikido is pioneering and still not mainstream in martial arts.

Trauma used to be something of a fringe interest, frankly. About ten years ago, I started sharing basics with groups I worked with, such as aid workers, soldiers and coaches. It seemed a huge blind spot. This took me to such places as Sierra Leone, Afghanistan and Ukraine. When I started working with yoga teachers, the general lack of trauma awareness shocked me – in particular, the disempowering "guru knows best" culture and the utter lack of consent for intrusive adjustments. Since then though, things have changed.

Celebrity trauma teachers however now pull in the crowds and £££€€€$$$s. Where "trauma sensitive" was once a polite request for professionals to increase their awareness and apply some basic consideration, more recently it's become a tyranny. This, combined with the diabolical "safe space" culture coming out of US universities (#triggered), makes me worry about where things are going.

Now, sensitivity is weaponised as a form of control, and victimhood is seen a virtue, if not a religion[41]. Being a "sensitive" teacher has gone beyond what UK law would call "making reasonable adjustments", to avoiding all activities that could be potentially upsetting for someone. Assuming basic grown-up resilience now makes you a bad person. Damaged people stalk the world acting as hurt tyrants. I feel sorry for them and hope they get help, but I won't be dictated to by them.

For many, the concept of "trauma" has spread to include merely being upset. Emotional "safety" is demanded. What the hell does that even mean? Where it means that a teacher shouldn't abuse or discriminate, then great, I'm with you 100%. However, it's started to mean that nobody can have an unpleasant emotion at any time. It's started to become synonymous with "offended" (another word used to control), and it's becoming a way to criticise all but the most egg-shell-walking teachers. I had a complaint once that there was a mirror in a training room I was using and I was called "trauma insensitive" for not covering it. Now, mirrors in a room aren't ideal from an embodiment perspective, but is it seriously that big a deal? If someone is literally scared of their own reflection, maybe they should be in 1-1 therapy and not in an educational environment for professionals! I assume basic adult robustness – this is reasonable.

There will no doubt be hysterical cries of "horrible mean man!" in response to this piece, also I'm not looking for sympathy here as that isn't a currency mature adults trade in. I'm not competing in the Sacred Victim Olympics. I do however understand trauma a little, both personally and professionally. I'd argue that the culture of making traumatised people almost holy, and insisting on unreasonable accommodation, doesn't help anyone. Also, when I work with people in genuinely unsafe environments, they have very little time for those co-opting these concepts and using them for social prestige and point scoring, which is the heart of this matter. A return to common sense, please!

---

41 Jonathan Haidt is excellent on this topic.

CAN WE BE *TOO* PRESENT?

Language is how we coordinate action over time and space, rather than through our embodiment. Language is how we get shit done, and while it always has an embodied component (we can be predisposed to "lean" towards "yes" or "no" for example) it is also more than this. Bodily mindfulness in the moment is not enough to be a functioning adult, so we should be a little cautious of embracing embodiment as the one complete answer to everything!

Embodiment and mindfulness enthusiasts need to work with linguistics because an obsession with the present moment can make people really bad at making commitments (promises of *future* action), declarations, keeping commitments (honour your word, hippie!) and generally organising stuff with other people. "Go with the flow" can be very low integrity, and the present moment can be a kind of comfortable trap, after a while.[42]

SLOW VERSUS FAST BODYMIND LEARNING

There are two roads to embodied learning: the long slow road and the short fast road. Both have pros and cons. As I was practicing aikido yet again last night (it's been 20+ years), I was reflecting on the beauty and depth of this long-term relationship, as well as the incredible ineffectual illogic of it!

The slow road is traditional embodied learning, like studying a Japanese martial art or a classic yoga form. You practise for many years, without explanation and little or no cultural or individual adaptation, and just randomly have insights (which you aren't given space to process). There's no explicit attempt to transfer the skills you learn into your daily life; the idea is that you just do enough of it and it becomes part of you. This type of practice isn't particularly goal driven and you pick it up mostly intuitively.

The advantages of this way of learning are that it's deep (working at the level of being), free flowing (which leads to unexpected wisdom),

---

42 Credit: This piece is influenced by ontological linguistics, which I encountered through both The Newfield Network and the Strozzi Institute.

richly embedded in a heritage that's part of the learning, and requires surrender and patience. The disadvantages are that you can waste a lot of time, be abused, deepen neuroses by picking the wrong practice in the first place, confuse the package for the essence, as it's all mixed up, and sometimes never get the life transfer (we all know the black-belt and flexible yogi arseholes).

The fast track means working very consciously around a clear aim, with modern teaching methods adapted to fit a particular group. In this way for example, I can teach a business group centring in 30–40 minutes, as opposed to the learning being embedded in years of aikido training. Very few people do this well yet, but it's emerging as an alternative to the long slow road.

The main advantage of the fast track method is that it works! It's practical. People today are busy, and rapid skill learning is extremely helpful to them. Real life transfer is often better with this method, as cultural trappings are stripped away and bridges to daily living are consciously built. This method avoids the sin of wasting people's precious time. Clarity of language and method is central here.

A disadvantage is that it may be somewhat shallow; the focused, goal-led nature means that the random fluctuations and confusions of a broader practise (often where the real gold lies) are missed. Another disadvantage of this method is that people may not value what is so accessible and clear. Climbing a mountain to meet a meditation guru and downloading an app in two minutes each lead to a very different practice commitment! Equally there is little community immersion, which is how a lot of the implicit lessons are socially "caught" in traditional learning. People learn from contact with people, even if that learning is not conscious.

Combining both is, of course, possible and wise. It's best done with a bit of integral, non-fundamentalist guidance in choosing one or two core, committed, old-school practices, supplemented with modern skills work to enhance and supplement them. One or two centres of excellence for embodied learning like this are now emerging – see for example Mile's Kessler's Integral Aikido Dojo in Tel Aviv. It's a dream of mine to create a centre where multiple traditional arts are taught with a modern embodied slant. In the meantime, educating students in this approach so that they can engage intelligently in whatever they do, is also effective.

PERCEPTUAL EMPATHY

Moods

It's obvious to most of us that we empathise with other people and can "catch" their moods. If you've ever, say, sat next to that angry guy on the train or been "infected" by the joy of children, you know that.

This effect is a part of how teaching yoga (or whatever) through demonstrating, works too. Watching a teacher actually primes your body for the movements, as you're mimicking them on a micro-level. Likewise, gentle physical strokes can serve as adjustments by merely "suggesting" direction to our bodies.

Moving objects

We can also catch embodied "instructions" from moving objects. We map pretty much anything onto ourselves, actually. We "taste" the world this way. The motion of whatever we see, or even just imagine, shapes us. For some nice examples, watch a plane take off, a waterfall cascade, or a cloud dissolve and feel this. This effect can be used deliberately.

Alexander Technique[43] teacher Bruce Fertman has done this by subtly opening our posture through looking at spheres moving like cogs. My local Alexander teacher Mark Claireaux does it by asking me to look at arrows on a picture. Paul Linden uses this effect in martial arts too; a high level aikidoka can unbalance you with empathy! I sometimes use it when I teach yoga; the gentle, natural quality of movement it can lead to is more desirable than the grosser "doing".

---

43 One of the earliest Western somatic approaches that works with posture and how we do whatever we do.

Shapes

In fact, we can all be seen as a subtle set of intentional directions. This is one way to look at character. So, it's more accurate to say our personality is a movement set that can be interfered with by other vectors (classic Paul Linden again). We're also subtly "instructed" by the shapes of our environments. Expansive views expand us, high ceilinged cathedrals ennoble us, straight lines and yoga mats cage us, and curves soften us. The places we live in enter us and influence our manner of being. Shapes shape us.

How do you find movements and environments influence you?

CHAPTER 10

MORE PERSONAL MOMENTS

Embodiment is by definition deep and personal, and perhaps a few more stories from my own life will help illustrate some key ideas in this book. Here are a few more snapshots and personal moments to conclude.

LOSE STRONG

– On the way to Poland, April 2017

People keep telling me to be strong. They mean the best of course, and I'd like to reply in a few ways.

The first is that I am strong and have worked on it. Thanks for the reminder. Twenty years of aikido, meditation, yoga, sobriety; volunteering with traumatised soldiers, kids, persecuted gay people; and generally staring at life's rougher side – wasn't for a fucking laugh. Neither the muscles nor the praise matter. What matters is being strong enough to speak at your father's funeral, or to make sure the work that you love doesn't suffer when you suffer. What matters is being strong enough to let your wife see you cry and let her be the big spoon for a while. Strength is spitting gratitude in the face of pain, humour in the face of despair, and celebration in the face of loss. This is strength. This is the muscle to build.

Another reply is: Please let me be weak now. That's if "strong" means having to be always on top of my shit, not feeling and not grieving; if it means denying the reality of heartbreak and the gift of deep mourning. Fuck you, if being strong means some loss-denying, positive thinking abomination. Life is about the shadows too, you sigh-puking, eye-contact-raping, white-wearing, spiritual by-passing motherfuckers. And fuck you, if being strong means some dictated, masculine ideal of invulnerability. Let me be weak for once. I've tested my courage and proven my worth. The salt in these tears doesn't answer to erectile insecurity.

Lastly, I'd reply that none of us are strong alone. As I've taught to aid workers in a dozen hellholes, we're inter-resilient. "I" is never, ever strong. "We" is strong. The myth of the lone, rugged individual in tough times just causes more suffering. In this spirit, I also deeply appreciate all the messages of support since my father died and the inter-strength of the remaining family. Special muscular hug to Polish Pete, who I was a live-in aikido student with, and who just lost his young wife Kasia to cancer. We slept on the floor, ate cheap food, had cold showers and were beaten senseless every night. Good times. Now these are bad times, and while we ain't quite as young, lean or mean now, we're still warriors. "This is what we trained for", he just said to me. Respect.

See you at her funeral, brother.

A KISS

I kiss all of her with all of me
I taste
The salt of her blood, sweat and tears
Between her legs

I kiss the body, with the body, as a body
A gentle respite for a cracked heart
Awareness bringing sweetness to this insulting march

I kiss all of her with all of me
Pleasure bringing life, bringing us home
To
One body

AS I TRAVEL HOME FROM MOSCOW . . .
– Moscow, December 2017

Many of us have felt like we don't matter. That we're not wanted. That we don't have a right to even exist. That we have no safe home.

Even with my confidence and bravado, this is true for me at times. For students with abuse histories and difficult personal backgrounds, it's usually true, and it's certainly present for people from persecuted groups. I was deeply touched last night when a member of the LGBTQ+ embodiment training in Moscow commented that the greatest gift of practise was simply to *be*. This is not a given for many people.

As someone who has been to the depths of alcohol abuse, survived dangerous countries, clinical depression, and lost many to suicide, *being* isn't a given. As someone lucky enough to finally be with his wife after recent visa trials, but who also not long ago, lost a father, it is also not a given to be with the ones that we love.

Sometimes a little yoga, martial arts or body meditation isn't so little; it's a stand for existence. So, let me dedicate this to the gift of being that practise constitutes, and to all those who struggle with this, whatever the threat.

"Give yourself the gift of being" may sound like some cheesy bullshit, but I mean this from my heart. To come home to the body is a defiant act of great courage and consequence. I support your right to be.

COMING TO LOVE THE ARCHETYPAL FATHER
– Cambridgeshire, May 2018

A lot of my life has centred on first fighting, then coming to love the archetypal father. In a feminised society, where boys are largely raised by women, and masculinity is mocked, repressed and despised by Hollywood and advertisers, this is a hard journey. The world now embodies the supposedly caring but tyrannical mother of both state and counterculture. She will look after you and keep you oh so safe. All she demands is your balls. It has become fashionable to, with ingratitude, blame "the patriarchy" (from the Greek for "rule of the father") for many horrors; but this is the most feminised time in recorded history. Whatever % of politicians or CEOs are men, this is not the age of men.

My teen years extended far into adult life, as I tried to kill Dad in many ways. And look at the state of the world – who wouldn't want to reject the norms of a sick society?! This anti-father urge is at the heart of so many of my "alternative" friends too, and they suffer for it. I came to love my father, but I was not well-raised to be a man by him. This sad fact is the norm – as is some alcoholism, on top of the usual lame, disempowered dad syndrome.

My adult life has also been about ways to re-father myself. The severe discipline of Japanese martial arts was excellent for this. I honour my many fathers there who initiated me, especially Don Levine, William Smith and Paul Linden senseis. I had to go to war zones and test my edge. My mother hated it but, to her credit, never tried to stop me. Taking on the challenges and responsibility of running a business aided further.

I also wonder if this re-fathering urge is in all those yogis lining up to be told what to do. And in all the lost hipsters dressing like lumberjacks, and sporting beards and tattoos. I see those looking to find meaning and ethics in the East. We long for manhood. We long for discipline, morals and responsibility, though they are almost dirty words now. Note: the arms of the far-right and Islamic extremists also await our youth who are seeking these things.

I was lucky enough to heal my relationship with my actual father before he died, and also with society. I see what is strong and beautiful about my nation and societal norms. I am married. My inner teen rebel is still strong, but the man behind him sits on the throne and smiles wryly. Thank you to all my fathers for not making this journey easy. The way of ease is the way of weakness.

My fathers have prepared me for the world. Thank you again.

THE THIRST NEVER LEAVES

The thirst that held my throat, and led me to the edge of suicide
while claiming to be my closest friend.
It cursed me alone in a crowded world
while embracing me warmly every night
Promising all
by delivering nothingness

That wrecked my body like a broken ship,
smashed on rocks of longing
Poisoned every cell so deeply that all life tasted of was nausea
That took everything

The thirst warped my heart and mind past measures
into the demon version of myself
Make no mistake, by the way . . .
the devil is a part of you just waiting to take charge
The true horror is that you will witness
the carnage you cause, helpless
A junkie will steal your wallet and then help you look for it.
The dregs of hope and care that remain, ensure the torture is total

The thirst took me places that I will not share for the shame
stooped my spine and sewed my eyes shut
And my parched throat tried to call out the names of the divine
But managed only to take another drink

I see now from the other side,

thirteen years sober by grace

That the thirst was my soul seeking love in all the wrong places

A mistaken shortcut to connection

to myself,

others

and The Mystery

The sheer stupidity of addiction is worth laughing at

That such smart people try to find spirit in spirits;

In a needle, in a stranger's arms, on social media, or whatever

In a way, it's a gift

To have a loaded gun at my head daily

That insists that I don't isolate

Insists that I do the work

That casually offers me a choice between

My wonderful life and a slow painful death

The devil inside says, "That beer looks refreshing.

One won't hurt."

And waits in the wings

I smile. Incline my face to the sun. And walk on

God's hand on my back.

Still

Thirsty

OLD AIKIDO FRIEND

Back grabbing my old aikido friend

Our dead teacher in both our bodies

I notice the first liver spots on my hand

Spring light and bird song outside

My knees ache a little more, but I also smile more fully

With each passing year and throw

RETURN TO THE ORDINARY
– Brighton, August 2019

I'm back from another trip to the wonderful unspectacular. Embodiment is often a similarly ordinary homecoming, not the fireworks of state-chasing that may first appeal, or the special exotic wisdom we sometimes imagine.

In the café, I enjoy not standing out. This isn't *Cheers*, not every-one knows my name and that's lovely. My wife is pleased to see me, of course, but doesn't unfurl a banner. She asks me to do the washing up and I do. The man at the corner shop has the same jokes. A traditional English curry still tastes good. How wonderful to return home to the everyday. This is where the real deal is – not on mountain tops, Goan beaches, or exciting workshops in Bali.

Giving up being special is a luxury. Prophets may have no honour at home, but wankers also get overly praised abroad. The body is ordinary. Magnificently so.

"Let It Be" comes on the radio.

MY GREED
– London, September 2019

Here are my professional embodiment goals:

- Reaching 100 million people on the Internet
- Training 100 facilitators to be better at this work than I am
- Making Embodied Yoga Principles (EYP) available as an option in major yoga studios in 1000 cities in 100 countries
- My grandchildren not understanding why my job existed

All these are well underway. Thank you for your support. "Success" isn't a dirty word.

AND, my ambition as an embodiment teacher, is also just to take a full healthy breath, before my breath moves on.

WE'RE ALL FROM THE SAME PLACE
– Berlin, January 2019

One grandfather soared in the air and dropped death on Germans. He screamed in his sleep until the day he died. The other was from a fishing village in Ireland. He spent his youth braving U-boats, sweating and shovelling coal in the bellies of warships to get his children to England. His wife held broken bodies from the war as a nurse, and later started a driving school – something as a woman she wouldn't have been able to do in Ireland at that time. She sent both her boys and girls to university, and cheated on her taxes. We're all trying to get somewhere. We're all immigrants.

My mother and father worked with drug addicts and many, many children. They ran a youth club for kids from West Indian families and ran interracial discos. She started the UK's first girls' football team. He cheered for Liverpool Football Club's first black player, while others threw bananas. He was on the wrong epilepsy drugs his whole life and drank too much, to quiet his head. She was a nun and ate the body of Christ, until they met. I joked with my dad that he was no saint. He's been dead a year now. I imagine his stooped body in a more peaceful place – though he was an atheist. I'll scatter his ashes on a hill in his hometown this weekend. We're all of the earth, eventually.

My cousin and dearest university friend both ended their own lives. I carried her body at her funeral and for a long time. I lit candles for them in Jerusalem, in the heart of a foreign religion. Sometimes, lighting a candle from another flame is all we can do. I dance with her often now, and fight with him from time to time. Bodies go into other bodies. Our dance passes on.

I married a girl from Ukraine. We met because of another war. Cousins break each other's bodies there, just like the Irish did. My best day's work was teaching ex-terrorists from both sides in Belfast – at the barracks my uncle was a soldier in during the Troubles. There, people ask you what side of the road you're from, to see if you're friend or foe. I travel the world, I've sweated in aikido dojos and yoga studios on five continents, and people of all nations come to me these days too. I joke with my quiet, Finnish student that my grandfather said they were good people to have on submarines. I flirt in Russian with an old woman who lived through communism. My grandfather used to sneak food and weapons past Hitler, from the USA, to her parents in the USSR. I train the first teacher in our system from the United States. Someone is speaking German and smiling. I imagine the beautiful children of a mixed-race couple on the course – they live as digital nomads and have more shades of lush brown between them than the fertile, farmland soil where I grew up. Who knows what colour eyes their kids will have, or what land they'll play in?

I cry the same sea tears as all of them, thinking of family sacrifice and pain. I fire-up the same red blood, like my grandfather in the furnaces. I think of the eyes of a sick Ashkenazi[44] mentor – "The same Jew eyes", Shakespeare or my mentor Don Levine might have said. I hear Paul Linden's voice making sick jokes about other kinds of furnaces that took members of his family. We reclaim what pain takes, with humour and with love. We need to keep learning this over again it seems. But eyes and hands can meet across the divides. We breathe the same air. Our feet all walk on the same earth. Until we enter it.

We're all from the body. We're all from the big body. We're all from the same place. Enough division.

THE BODY OF MATURITY

– I'm 40. Rural East Anglia.

In the flat green field James hugs me. A smelly man hug, the likes of which you can only have after many years of friendship. He's a carpenter and reeks of weed and work. His hands are like gnarled wisdom, his face looks ten years older than mine, but our birthdays are days apart, and we've known each other since we were both three. Now we're having our 40th birthday party together. I've come home.

James' kids and partner Kate hug me. They're excited to see cool uncle Mark and pull on my legs. I've been bringing them cool shit from around the world from my work travels for some years. I usually get the oldest, John, knives and skulls and things he loves and hides from his mum.

---

44 From the Hebrew word "Ashkenaz", referring to Germany, and a member of the Jews who lived in the Rhineland valley and in neighbouring France before their migration eastward to Slavic lands.

Daria is here of course too. She hides behind her long dark hair, as the party develops. She can be confident when she needs to be, and is sure tough, but she's an introvert kitty at heart. She slinks between the shadows and avoids the fuss. She has one paw somewhere else, but will hold me human enough, as she has on many nights now. We heal in love, nothing else.

My sister is here smiling and my niece runs ahead and demands "upside-down hugs" (where I pick her up and spin her around), which are getting more difficult as she gets bigger! I try and be a good influence in her life. We both have ADHD, it turns out. She loves me and I her.

Some colleagues from The Embodied Facilitator Course are here. Some are not, I piss too many people off with my drive and honesty . . . and the Russians couldn't make it due to visas, but Lee and Karin are here. He's a big bearded men's group leader and she's a softly spoken Dutch Buddhist. They seem to be sharing a tent this weekend . . . interesting. I smile. We've done a lot of good work together . . . really changed some lives. God knows how we've kept the business afloat for 13 years now! People are starting to regard me as a grown-up and no longer the *enfant terrible* now, I hear.

I'm still sober of course. I note that my wife and I don't argue like my parents did. She hints to a story from the Ukraine that doesn't bear telling. Generation by generation things can get better.

There are a lot of people here and a lot not. Many people that I grew up with are present with their kids. Same faces but with fewer lines. I blow Sally, Kasia and Rachel a kiss on the wind, and tip my glass of juice to my dad, to William Smith Sensei and to Don Levine. I feel them all in me. I've come home. I hug Daria again. I breathe. I'm glad we made it.

RESOURCES

There are a range of resources and trainings available if you want to learn more about embodiment. If you've enjoyed this book, the first thing I recommend is to go to www.TheEmbodimentBook/extras to get an extra chapter, listen to interviews on the writing process and get my newsletter to hear about future books (there's already another more or less done, and a third one half written). I have also written several e-books, some of which are freely available online (available for download from www.embodiedfacilitator.com)

If you're a facilitator looking for embodiment training, see the Embodied Facilitator Course (EFC), which runs annually (www.embodiedfacilitator.com). If you're a yoga teacher, you may be interested in Embodied Yoga Principles (EYP) training (www.embodiedyogaprinciples.com).

I also recommend books and courses from the influences I've mentioned:

- *Dylan Newcomb*
- *Ginny Whitelaw*
- *Paul Linden*

- *Richard Strozzi-Heckler*
- *Stuart Heller*
- *Wendy Palmer*

I have made more videos than I can remember (these are available on my YouTube channel: www.youtube.com/user/IntegrationTraining), and have recorded various workshops and webinars that you can buy at the EFC site. It is often easier to see and hear embodiment techniques on video than to explain them in print so I recommend this medium for actual techniques.

Many of the ideas presented here are also fleshed-out on my podcast, The Embodiment Podcast (freely available at www.embodiedfacilitator.com/the-embodiment-podcast, as well as on iTunes and the usual platforms). Podcast episodes feature me and a host of guests talking about various aspects of embodiment, as well as solo episodes and are great if you like learning on the move.

I also lead The Embodiment Conference, a massive online event, which features many facilitators from a range of embodiment fields. Easy to Google.

Finally, if you're interested in accessible, in-person, peer-to-peer embodiment training, see if there are any 'Embodiment Circles' near you (www.embodimentcircle.com).

ABOUT THE AUTHOR

Mark Walsh has dedicated his life to embod-
ied learning. He founded the Embodied
Facilitator Course (EFC), Embodied Yoga
Principles (EYP) and Europe's first embodied business training company, Integration
Training. He has taught in fifty countries and
made embodiment available online through
a YouTube channel with over 14 million hits.
More recently, he founded The Embodiment
Podcast, and in 2018, launched the ground-
breaking Embodiment Conference, which
was attended by over 15,000 people (and 150,000+ are expected in
2020). He has also published articles on numerous websites, such as
Elephant Journal, and been featured on many podcasts. As a speaker,
he has keynoted the International Coach Federation's annual UK conference, and spoke at Moscow State University psychology department.

He has an honours degree in psychology, an aikido black-belt and
has trained with various body-mind masters and in many approaches,
including yoga (for 25 years), NonViolent Communication, Feldenkrais,
conscious dance, Being-In-Movement, Improv, MMA, Leadership
Embodiment, body psychotherapy and meditation.

Generally, these days he dedicates himself to teaching other facilitators and mentoring young embodiment teachers, but his past clients
include IKEA, Unilever, L'Oréal, Virgin Atlantic, AXA, Shell, Sussex
University and The House of Lords. He has also worked in peace and

trauma projects in Israel/Palestine, Afghanistan, Ukraine, the slums of Brazil, East Africa and with the Sierra Leonian Army.

Based in Brighton UK, he likes cats, curry, his wife Daria, and feels ridiculous writing about himself in the third person.

www.facebook.com/mark.walsh.9256
www.instagram.com/warkmalsh
www.twitter.com/warkmalsh/@warkmalsh

APPENDIX

– Beyond mindfulness?

While it makes for a snappy title, I have some caution in presenting the idea of embodiment being 'beyond mindfulness', or of presenting mindfulness as just being aware of a body. It is, however, unfortunately, presented like that in various lightweight modern secular expressions, and there are some body-hating parts of traditional Buddhism (which recommend seeing the body as nothing more than a decaying corpse for example), so it is still a fair subtitle.

There is, however, a richer tradition of how mindfulness meets bodily experience and this is worth noting, to be fair and balanced. In some texts, the explicit foundational practice of everything that comes under the umbrella of mindfulness – as laid out in the *Satipathana sutta* for example – is to establish embodied awareness (*yonisomanisikara*), literally 'womby' attention; attention that suffuses bodily experience, grounded in the belly centre. This is explicitly much more intimate and integrated than just being aware of the body. The first foundation of mindfulness practice is called *kayanupassana,* which we can translate as 'tracking bodily experience', and which the Buddha repeatedly expresses as 'knowing bodily experience from the inside'. Sometimes 'knowing the body in the body' is a translation from the Pali that sounds very much embodied. Traditional Buddhism could, therefore, be argued to be much closer to an embodied approach, despite some very anti-body quotes in early Buddhist texts. Later Buddhism likewise includes both strong body-celebrating elements (e.g. in Tibetan Buddhism and some forms of Zen), as well as transcendent elements that see the body as nothing more than meat to rise above. Equally some early yoga texts can be seen to be very embodied (especially from tantric traditions), while others very anti-body (e.g. some verses from Patanjali's famous yoga sutras).

All this being said, we could still refer back to the fundamental skill-set of embodiment as bodily awareness and choice. This means that we are not just mindful of the body, even in a richer sense of this term, but also alter it. Embodiment is sensory *and* motor, so can, therefore, be rightly said to be more than mindfulness, if we follow a commonly used modern definition of mindfulness being 'non-judgmental present moment awareness'. Embodiment is, at heart, much more active. As ever, traditions are varied and much comes down to definitions, and while there is a gentle provocation in the book's subtitle, it is not a dig at Buddhism or deeper practitioners of modern mindfulness.

Thanks to my Buddhist teacher friend Martin Aylward for his challenge around this and help with this section.

POSTSCRIPT

This poem brings together much of the book in a beautiful if somewhat anarchic form. It is a poetic "mash-up" containing quotes, inspiration and paraphrases from a range of sources, including Walt Whitman, a traditional New Guinean saying, Mary Oliver, James Joyce, George Leonard, Rumi, The Koran, Sonya Renee Taylor, Thich Nhat Hanh, Dylan Newcombe, Gabrielle Roth, Francis Briers, Emilie Conrad, Madeline Aguire, Nandita Muni, Nietzsche, Buddha, Jesus, The Katha Upanishad, Samuel Beckett, St Teresa, Aboodi Shabi, Stuart Heller, Renee Boyer-Willisson, Jewel Mathieson and more!

Note: If I included something you've said about the body and not named you forgive me, I honestly forget where I heard things and it all mingles together.

I SING THE BODY IN THE ELECTRIC AGE

I sing the body in the electric age.

I sing the body in the age of over-information,
miseducation and enter-braindrainment.

I sing the body organic, sustainable and unfairly-traded,
for a world gone mad on mind;

a cognitive catastrophe of un-noticing,
a blinding of the great eye of feeling.

I sing the body electric

while the subtle pulse of nature risks overwhelm

and we live an ever-increasing short distance from our bodies.

I sing beyond the body as more than just a brain taxi

beyond a thing that we own

that transports a bloated knowing, controlling and fearing . . .

I sing of a field of flesh

beyond right and wrong

as the ONLY place where we can meet

and I pray that we meet there!

I sing the body electric in an age where food is

often more toxin than nutrition;

where fundamentalists still make the fundamental mistake

of making our fundamental bodily foundation the foe

where we're trying to be sensational celebrities

without coming to our senses sensibly

where we have traded our basic interface with reality

and basic core operating system

for pale digital denizen denigration.

There is more wisdom in the body

than in any book or any philosophy.

So don't believe a word I say

and feel for yourself.

There is no higher authority than intimacy, intuition and irreverence.

Auto-anaesthesia is literally killing us,

as how we relate to the ourselves, is how we relate to each other,

other is how we relate to the planet.

How we relate to ourselves
is how we relate to each other
is how we relate to the planet.

The body is life.
We only feel when we move
and we only know we're alive when we feel.

Health IS movement.
Sickness is unfeeling and stuckness.
Life IS movement;
when we die, we stop. When we stop we die.

We do not express ourselves through movement –
we ARE ourselves through movement.

We are human movings, not human doings.

Movement is what we are, not something that we do.

We dance first, think later – that is the natural order.

If you want to move your mind, move!
If you want to move someone, move!
If you want to move the world, move!

Education that sits us in rows
and removes movement and play and life
is not education, but only the
indoctrination of unconscious conformity.

Knowledge is only a rumour
until it is in the muscle!

What children learn in schools is not to BE;

not wisdom, or relationships, or about themselves,

but how to know, know, know;

how to own, how to grasp, and how to do, do, do!

I sing in a world where body parts are more offensive than poverty

or bigotry;

where describing the sweetness of the otter's pocket

could deprive this book of liberty!

Nonsense,

There is nothing as sacred

as the doors of the great womb from which we are birthed –

your mama and great earth mama's mama!

And I know my work here is done

when lovers will whisper what are now obscenities

into each other's sacred orifices

tenderly,

into the night . . . with shame only a faded nightmare of

a long forgotten land

I sing where the standard world of working

shackles us to one folded posture,

arms handcuffed to a keyboard

eyes bound in the hard stare of fear and anger

straight ahead at the screen;

where clothes make women contorted and unstable

and put a noose around men's necks,

where the body has become the frozen valley of the shadow of life.

I sing the body electric because the promise of ease

has become the lie of sloth

because the dream of technology

has become the nightmare of roboticism

because where spirit once roared through the human body,

it now whimpers,

afraid to dance a defiant chorus of feeling.

The body is a gateway to God

and if you want to truly shake with spirit,

you must first shake your arse,

and maybe someone else's too!

Christ has no body but yours

and he prays with his hands, heart and tongue.

If you want to talk with tongues

you must first entangle them

because grace is, well,

graceful!

And if you want to get zen

you have to get down.

Of what is the body made?

it is made of emptiness, of rhythm and of nothing. Of no *thing*.

At the heart of the world

there is no solidity

there is only the dance.

Our bodies tell our story

in tension, gait and posture;

We move through space like we move through life.

Our stance is our stance to life.

We lean towards, well . . . what we lean towards.

Every wrinkle tells a story

and how we live is determined and broadcast

every moment in fleshy form.

We don't just need vagina monologues

but full body dialogues. Full. Body. Dialogues

When we listen and talk

and then listen some goddamn more! With our WHOLE bodies

peace is not just possible

but inevitable!

Peace is not just possible

but inevitable.

Peace is built into the body.

It is how the body works at its best.

God has ploughed peace into our blueprint, if we only listen.

I am not the body of magazine covers

or skeleton clothes hanger

who would snap if a man ever took them in his arms

and ravished them senseful.

I am not the body of posing black and white, un-souled men

with the tight bodies of fear and self-judgement.

I am not the body of the airbrushed, branded and made

"Mc-me" consumer object.

But I am the body fiercely sexual and proud!

And stop that tittering at the back.
We are not embarrassed children
your shame is violence, not sex.
The body is our gateway to God
the original mystic
the prophets of all religions listen to.

All bodies have one heart that beats
and it is the heart of the divine.

This body of ours is a temple
and God is nearer to us
than our jugular vein.

Open thy hand and know thou art love.

The soul's detest of violence
is built into the very fabric of the flesh;
only through not feeling ourselves
can we hurt another.

Values are visceral.
My body avoids the religious middlemen
and they're usually men
but more uptight than middling,
the middlemen who deny and repress the body
lest their flock get their truth straight from the source
and they lose their percentage, their control and their fearmongering.

The body is anchored in the here and now
while the mind travels to the past and the future.
Mindfulness is impossible without bodyfulness!
And sweat is as good a prayer as any that insulted silence.

Behind your thoughts

there is a wolf growling.

Behind your thoughts

there is a lover whispering,

and a prophet preaching.

The body is NOT an apology.

My body, you had me at "yes!"

My body, you saved me at "no!"

The way we treat our bodies, each other, and the planet are one.

In the body is the truth that we are one.

We start connected

connected through our bodies umbilically,

and we lose our little selves

in the big booty of being.

The body is holographic and umbilical in nature.

If you're not in your body, you are homeless

and there is no alternative.

Let's get involved and evolved.

This is commonsensual!

To touch

is to be touched

is to be, touch.

I do not just sing about my body,

because there is but one body.

I am in you

and you are in me.

We mingle like artists' paint
in a plasmic puddle
until the colour is nought but rainbow
and the self is pure light.

We are porous and connected
more wave than particle
more verb than noun
more process than product.

I am the body starving in East Africa
I am the body of the sex-trafficked victim
and her best friend
that holds her body as she cries.

I am the body of the molester behind bars
and politician in a prison of lies

I am the body of the Israeli and the Palestinian
the banker and the beggar.

I am the body of all people,
or none.

I beseech you
You only have to show up at the feast of your own life
right here;
the church, library and playground are one
and the doors are wide open!

You only have to let the soft animal of your body
love what it loves.
You only have to let the soft animal of your body
love what it loves.

We have come to be danced

where the kingdoms collide

in the cathedral of flesh

to burn back into the light

to unravel

to play

to fly

to root in skin sanctuary and muscular ministries.

We have come to be danced.

And in the end

words fail and fall

like dead leaves from the supple oak of our bodies

And all I have to say is. . . . thank you.

More Gratuitous praise

"Mark Walsh has more breadth of experience than anyone I know in the embodiment field, which makes this a passionate, authoritative and damn useful little book for anyone wanting to get a sense of what it's all about, or get some inspiration for an already established practice. Worth reading for the deeply personal stories and poems woven through, too."

— Adam Barley, founder of ZeroOne movement practice

"Mark has a special ability to make embodiment work relevant and accessible. This down to earth book is inspiring & informative to anyone with a body and an interest in engaging it to make this world a better place."

— Arawana Hayashi, co-founder of Social Presencing Theater, Presencing Institute

"Mark has a vision, and also has the energy and drive to make it happen. His commitment is to help everyone return home to their body. This is a huge undertaking. This books gently informs you and surprises you as you begin to do your part."

— Betsy Polatin, movement and breathing specialist, and author of "Humanual"

"Mark Walsh is one of the most committed embodiment learners and teachers I know. This book is an authentic, heartfelt treatise and handbook for how to live a more embodied life. Highly recommended."

— Curtis Watkins, somatic coach

"This work is a valuable asset to how we navigate life. Practical, applicable, to the point and makes us consider who we are and the effect of our place in any community."

— Gary Carter, yoga and anatomy teacher

"This book is a potpourri of ideas and personal reflections on the concept and nature of embodiment. Mark Walsh fertilises our sense of being, who we are and how we connect to each other and the planet. He brings an honesty and perceptive thread to the discourse on inter-corporeality. This book has a richness of scents and resources for those of us with a thirst to dwell in our subjective bodies as a way of becoming".

— Professor Helen Payne, PhD, registered ADMP UK, UKCP, University of Hertfordshire, author

"Mark Walsh brings an informed, passionate perspective out into the world. His down to earth musings, and targeted checklists, especially for facilitators, generate easily digestible food for thought and a call to action. Even though our social/political opinions diverge significantly at moments, we share a mutual focus: the liberation of the body and its full expression in society."

— Jamie McHugh, somatic movement specialist and artist

"Accessible, pithy, and engaging, captures Mark's distinctive voice, a compressive overview of such an invaluable subject."

— Jayaraya, Buddhist teacher, writer and mindful communication blockhead, dude, guru-coach-trainer

"Mark Walsh is much more than a writer, he "walks the talk" of embodiment with courage and humility. This book is as refreshingly honest, provocative and insightful as the man himself. Highly recommended to anyone engaged in the subversive act of reinhabiting their own bodily truth."

— John Cremer, author of "Improv" and "The Art of Reading People", Speaker of the Decade – The Academy of Chief Executives

"Mark has written both a scary book and a profound book for everyone who has a body. The scary part will expose you to how disembodiment happens and the consequences, the profound part will guide you to becoming reembodied as well as pointing out all the benefits that accrue when you have done that. As someone who's been engaged in this work for the past three decades, I can say you won't find a more direct manual on how to reengage your body."

— Joseph Riggio, cognitive scientist, master NLP trainer, designer of the MythoSelf® Process

"Reading through Mark's book was for me like sitting in nature for a day: some quiet moments, some raucous ones, and glimmers of gold. Mark's depth of practice and experience alone make me want to read what he writes, and this particular form – a short book with digestible chapters – makes it a gracious entry point for those wanting to explore the subject."

— Liam Bowler, host of The Body Awake podcast, bodyworker

"Mark's writing is perfectly aligned with who he is and how he teaches: forthright and honest, clear and helpful, fearless and with plenty of heart. His reflections offer both direct instruction for a more embodied, empowered and enlightened life, and an impactful, personal account of his own deepening transformation through the practices he teaches, and has made the centre of his life."

— Martin Aylward, meditation teacher and author

"Mark is by turns challenging, insightful and compassionate in his writing and coaching of embodiment. For the martial artist, his approach will give you tools, strategies and a clear path to better understanding the true natur of Martial Arts: to, "know thyself". This book is highly recommended."

— Matt Hill, Systema instructor, author, aikido sensei

"Perhaps the greatest sickness of our time is the disconnection between body and mind. Not only does this affect our health and wellbeing, but it disconnects us from our inner nature and the natural world around us. We don't need to look far to see the grave consequences of this. Mark clearly highlights these issues and gives the reader some great pointers towards reconnection and embodiment. This book will give encouragement to anyone who has a body."

– Michael Kern, biodynamic craniosacral therapist, founder of the Craniosacral Therapy Educational Trust, and author of "Wisdom In The Body"

"No other person has had a bigger impact reclaiming "embodiment" for the mainstream as Mark Walsh. In his new book, Mark compassionately shares embodiment with a disembodied world, in a way that is pithy, personal, and profoundly relatable. Mark makes embodiment as accessible as reaching around and grabbing your own ass with both hands. I say get this book and cop a feel!"

– Miles Kessler, meditation teacher, aikido sensei, director of The Integral Dojo

"Mark has established himself as a significant player in the world of embodied movement, and in this book we can understand why. Part autobiography, part discourse, he uses his life to illustrate how we become fragmented and how we can become whole again. Through poetry, bullet points and streams of consciousness he provokes, implores, and cajoles us to move, feel and respond fully to life."

– Peter Blackaby, yoga teacher, author of "Intelligent Yoga"

"Mark Walsh's work is a recognition of the body as the site of being, and an extremely well-articulated guide to how to reconnect to the body. Mark's work has provided an invaluable guideline to how to generalise insights from physical practice to life in general that has been incredibly valuable for my own work. I had been friends with Mark for years before I attended his course, I knew him as an irreverent, confrontational, lighthearted and brilliant character; but discovered his teaching was far more powerful than I expected. I am super grateful for my friendship with Mark and the deeply enlightening work he is sharing with the world."

– Rafe Kelley, founder of Evolve Move Play

Our times are wild, wonderful, weird and warped. We are both the luckiest people who have ever lived and the most alienated, confused and overwhelmed. A "consensus trance" dumbs us down, but we can awaken from it in many ways. None is more immediate and tangible than awakening from the pervasive illusion that has so many lost in thought, imagining the body radically separate from consciousness and all that is sacred. Mark Walsh recognized this as an enormous opportunity, and he has seized upon it with zeal, gusto and wide-ranging intelligence. In *Embodiment*, he gives voice to a joyous, angry, sensual war-cry – the body ferociously reclaiming its primacy in a disembodied world.

– Terry Patten, author, "A New Republic of the Heart", co-author "Integral Life Practice"

Printed in Poland
by Amazon Fulfillment
Poland Sp. z o.o., Wrocław